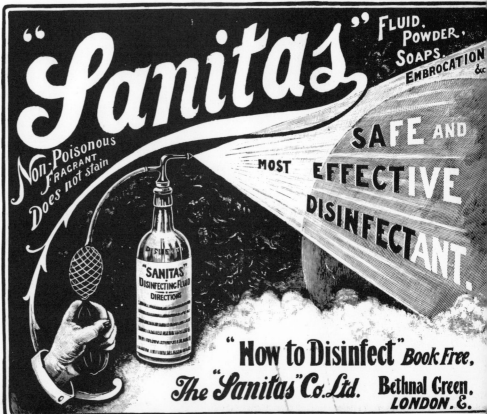

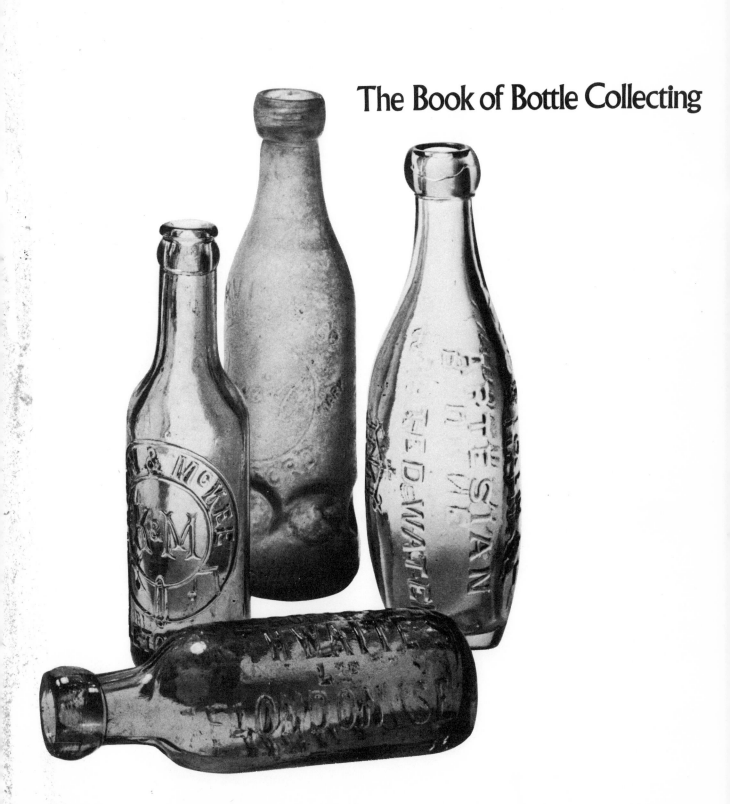

The Book of Bottle Collecting

The Book of

Bottle Collecting

Doreen Beck

Hamlyn   London · New York · Sydney · Toronto

published by
The Hamlyn Publishing Group Limited
London · New York · Sydney · Toronto
Hamlyn House, Feltham, Middlesex, England

© copyright
The Hamlyn Publishing Group Limited 1973

First edition 1973
Second impression 1974

ISBN 0 600 31310 7

Printed in U.S.A.

(title-page) Mineral water bottles. (Roy
Morgan Collection).

Contents

2 Some collectors make a point of hunting for bottles on the sea shore after a storm. These bottles were washed up on the Kent coast at Sandwich after the floods of 1953.

Introduction

Who would have thought that bottles would become the object of a cult?—those ordinary, glass containers which have been solving some kind of storage problem ever since humans first learned how to make them somewhere in ancient Egypt or maybe it was Mesopotamia more than 1000 years BC.

Curiously enough an Italian word for bottle is *fiasco*. Our usage of that word was borrowed from the colloquial phrase *far fiasco*, literally *to make a bottle*, but having the sense of making a mess of something. The phrase seems to have been connected at an early date with events on the stage, but its origins remain somewhat obscure. One interesting theory is that in the heyday of glass-making in Venice, any piece which did not make the grade as a fine goblet or vase was called a bottle. It is not a bad theory. The crudest kind of glass has long been referred to as bottle glass.

For a brief period in early eighteenth-century France it seems that gourmets were persuaded that their wine would be more delicate and delicious taken from crude forest glass—another name for bottle glass. But the snobbery has usually been the other way round.

The aristocratic and decorative members of the bottle family—decanters, snuff and scent bottles, for example—have of course long been included in the ranks of the blessed, in the fine as opposed to the common glass category. They are proudly displayed in museums and private collections and written about at length in most books concerned with the history of glass. But ordinary household bottles? Are they not, after all, appropriately damned as common containers?—and though invaluable, rightly taken for granted by the average householder?—and given short shrift by most writers considering the wonders of the glass-maker's art? A rapidly growing number of people in the United States of America and increasingly in Britain, Canada, Australia and New Zealand, think not.

Modern design has had considerable impact on kitchen containers—among other things—and many an *un*-common glass bottle or jar now elegantly displays spices and spaghetti and coffee beans and sugar and sauces and syrups. But except for those with a passion for contemporary design these are not generally the objects of the bottle collector's hunt.

The bottle boom that has been taking place in the United States of America in the last decade or so and has spread further afield is, in fact, taken up with the common and not-so-common old bottle. Unlike many if not most collecting passions, however, this

7

3 This diver has found a Roman stoneware amphora. Glass bottles of Roman and more recent times can be discovered on many coasts.

4 A model of a glasshouse built in the Surrey Weald in the fourteenth century. Glassmakers worked in the woods which supplied the furnaces with fuel and a source of potash. This continued until coal began to replace wood in the early seventeenth century. In 1615 the use of wood-fuel was prohibited. (Pilkington Glass Museum, St Helens, Lancashire).

one is not just concerned with the relics of yesteryear—nor with paying out good money 'for them fool furrin bottles what can't set up'. The pre-1900 vintage, both American and foreign, does have a very strong following, but more recent converts are collecting more recent vintages, including such pop art objects as Coca-Cola bottles and such humble witnesses of bygone domesticity as preserving bottles, or fruit jars as they are usually called in America, not to mention the glass specialities favoured by some whisky distributors and the latest perfume bottles off the Avon assembly line, all designed with the collector in mind. The bottle-collecting market has become so large that some manufacturers are actually selling bottles with nothing in them, simply as decorative items that will never be filled, at least not with anything edible. All the bottles specially designed with the collector in mind are, in fact, changing the nature of collecting from one long tramp into a virtual armchair occupation. But they are only incidentally the subject of this book.

Under an old criterion, the desirability of any object from a collector's point of view is determined by its aesthetic appeal and its rarity, linked whenever possible to the intriguing historic associations that bring to life any object out of the past.

That anyone should consider collecting common bottles for their beauty is reason enough for incredulity, not to say blank incomprehension—at least to the uninitiated. Yet simple bottles have often been singled out for shapeliness or colour or some other quality that charms the eye. The tears that are controlled in sophisticated ware often appear as accidental flaws in common bottles, for example, and are no less enchanting for being haphazard. In our own age of super-self-service stores, the visual attraction, or rather attractiveness, of glass containers has helped to sell many a product. Look again, all ye unbelievers!

With the rapid substitution of paper cartons, plastic and aluminium for glass in kitchen and bathroom at the present time, glass containers are gaining in rarity value as well as in historic, or as it is sometimes called, antiquarian interest. I hazard the guess that maybe the desire to find and preserve such common containers as milk bottles is, in fact, a reaction against the throw-away mentality of the last few decades, a revolt against the built-in obsolescence of recent manufacturing, and to paraphrase that early seventeenth-century sage, Francis Bacon, just another effort to rescue something from the flux of time.

Bottles have been preserved for thousands of years,

5 American commemorative whisky flask of mould-blown glass showing a horsedrawn railroad car with the inscription 'Success to the Railroad'. These flasks are much sought after today. (Private Collection).

of course, but usually for economic reasons. Until the early part of the twentieth century, they were relatively expensive to make and were saved for constant re-use. Some were re-cycled—long before that word became a contemporary cliché—but happily for those now engaged in the systematic and specialised search for old and not-so-old bottles, not all glass containers disappeared that way. Future collectors looking for the common containers of today might have a harder time, particularly if the philosophy which calls for the constant re-use of all materials is ever put into operation. As it is, the re-cyclers have discovered that ground glass is excellent for land fill, as a soil conditioner and as an aid in trash incineration processes. Better collect today what may not survive tomorrow!

Soaring interest in bottles has brought with it the inevitable rash of fakes and reproductions. One famous American calabash bottle—the gourd-shaped bottle with a long slender neck—made in commemoration of a two-year tour through the country in the 1850s by the Swedish singer, Jenny Lind, and embossed with the lady's portrait, was actually counterfeited in Czechoslovakia some years ago. And many a fake has been planted in the barns and henhouses of New England to trap unwary antique hunters scouring around for bargains. It is the old collectors' law of demand and supply, so watch out!

A famous set of Canopic jars—used by the ancient Egyptians to preserve the entrails of embalmed bodies—was acquired by the British Museum in London early in this century. They were considered unusual because they were made of glass. Careful examination, however, revealed that the glass was of recent manufacture, and that the jars were, in fact, clever fakes made from moulds taken from genuine vessels in the more usual pottery.

Since more and more people are searching for bottles 'of every description' in the words of the nineteenth-century bottle manufacturers' advertising copy, the sophisticated trick is also to make sure that yours once did contain wine or whisky or beer or soda-water or ink or pickles or perfume, and were not churned out last week as decorator's items in Japan, Denmark, Great Britain or the United States of America. The armchair collector should certainly want to make sure that the moulds for his speciality in whisky or perfume bottles have been destroyed as the manufacturers are promising, and that some rarity value is thereby assured for his or her purchases.

If a Bill now before Congress is ever passed, it could become illegal to both manufacture and import

6 A group of cobalt and copper blue
bottles most of which contained poisons.
The smallest bottle in the foreground is
just over 1¼ inches (3·3 cm.) high.
(Roy Morgan Collection).

reproductions without a date of manufacture permanently embossed on them.

The more respectable reproductions do that already, or are accompanied by certificates of limitation and an edition number or other mark of identification.

The Wheaton-Nuline Glass Company of New Jersey, for example, which has recreated an entire glass-making village, issues limited editions of American Presidential flasks, for example, modelled on those of the early nineteenth century. On the occasion of their tenth anniversary in 1969, which coincided with the hundredth anniversary of the completion of the trans-continental railroad, the Antique Bottle Clubs Association in California issued replicas of the mid nineteenth-century flask which celebrated the joining of the tracks from the east and west coasts in Utah in 1869. The toast embossed on the flasks appropriately

5 enough was: 'Success to the Railroad'. A facsimile of an eighteenth-century wine bottle was recently issued in Britain in commemoration of the Silver Wedding Anniversary of Queen Elizabeth II and Prince Philip.

There have been many superstitions associated with glass through the ages, which is really not so surprising when you think of the marvel of transmuting 'dust and sand (for they are the only main ingredients) to such a diaphanous, pellucid, dainty body as you see a Crystal-Glass is'—the kind of necromancy which so caught the imagination of an English visitor to Venice in the early seventeenth century. There was more to it than met the eye, of course, but the wonder has remained even for bottle glass, which may be neither pellucid nor dainty. In the nineteenth century the basic structure of glass began to be understood, and it has since been shown that there are hundreds of thousands of different types of glass, or glasses as the scientists would prefer, each with its own characteristic properties and chemical composition, just as is true of ceramics, metals and textiles. In fact, the structure of glass is so enormously varied, that even today there is technical discussion among scientists as to what glass really is.

There is in addition a certain anonymity about glass-makers that contributes not a little to the mystery that surrounds the material they work with.

Glass-makers were a roving bunch. They almost had to be, since they were constantly searching for fuel to keep the furnaces burning. That meant that

4 most glass-houses were built in or near forests, wood being the principal fuel until well into the nineteenth century, even after the discovery and exploitation of

coal for the purpose. The derogatory term, 'rough forest glass', synonymous with bottle glass, derives from the location of the early glass-houses. More sophisticated craftsmen set up shop in towns or near wealthy patrons and imported their fuel. But they too were given to wandering. The skills developed in one place were coveted elsewhere and skilled workers, who could escape tyrannical masters, moved to wherever there was a demand for their labour. The results of that labour were exported far and wide and it is often hard to say just where any piece in a given style was produced. In the eighteenth and nineteenth centuries, glass-makers wandered across the Atlantic from the major glass-producing countries, principally Britain and Germany, but also Italy, Spain and France, just as in previous centuries they had emigrated from one European country to another in search of employment for their talents.

The cloak of anonymity has not yet been penetrated by chemical analysis or any other scientific effort to provide fool-proof evidence of origin. The recipes for making glass, even in the smallest glass-houses, have been shown to vary so much, that it is impossible to identify with any certainty the products of one house, let alone a whole region. Other historical evidence is needed before even an educated guess is possible.

Interest in certain types of bottles found in America – notably the delightful, round and fat, little, diamond-patterned scent bottles or flasks made around the turn of the eighteenth century, and the pocket or whisky flasks, embossed with such patriotic emblems as the American eagle and the heads of George Washington and subsequent Presidents of the Republic in the first half of the nineteenth century – dates back to the 1920s and was part of the burgeoning curiosity about American arts and crafts in general that was taking place at the time.

Startling as it may now seem, when some thought was being given to establishing the first English colony at Jamestown, Virginia, in the very early years of the seventeenth century, glass-making was mentioned as a promising way of making money – promising, that is, if you forgot about the hardships involved in settling a wilderness and risking starvation, not to mention attacks from hostile Indians, in order to build a glass-house. The venture, not surprisingly, was not a success, but glass-making had achieved the honour of being the first type of manufacturing attempted on these shores. Later attempts, up and down the eastern seaboard and westward with the expanding nation, were more successful, and bottle-making, along with

window glass, was the principal business of the day. Fancier ware was strictly after-hours or off-hand work, as it is called, until well into the nineteenth century. And, lest we forget, bottle-houses had been in business in various parts of the British Isles long before George Ravenscroft set English and Irish glass-making on a more aristocratic road towards the end of the seventeenth century.

Bottle collecting as an organised hobby was started in California in 1959 when a handful of people got together in Sacramento to form the first bottle-collecting club. Since that time, they have made thousands of converts, and there are now more than one hundred clubs across the country, at least one in Canada, one in Britain and one in Australia. And although old favourites are still sought after, the new focus of interest is on the more utilitarian household bottles and jars which proliferated during the nineteenth century.

Most bottles available to the collector are from the late nineteenth and twentieth centuries. Very few in either high or humble style have survived from the 2 centuries prior to that. But there is still a lot of digging and diving going on among ancient ruins and on ocean 3 bottoms, so it is not as unlikely as it first sounds to conceive of recently formed collections of Roman bottles, for example.

More recent sources are local rubbish dumps, construction holes, the sites of former glass-houses, ghost-towns, old farmsteads, breweries, wayside pubs (in Britain), saloons and illicit stills from the Prohibition era in America. Anyone in the vicinity of the Panama Canal could take an intriguing bottle-hunting hike along Las Cruces trail, a cobblestone path through the jungle from the old town of Las Cruces to Panama City. The bottles to be found along that way might have been dropped off by the forty-niners on their way to the California gold fields in 1849, or much earlier by Spaniards escorting gold and silver trains across the Isthmus on the last stretch of the long trek up from Peru to the Caribbean terminus, or by Sir Francis Drake and his crew who lay in wait for them, or by Henry Morgan and his pirates who did likewise. A considerable amount of diving is going on in the same area and yielding not a few early wine and spirits bottles among others.

Standard equipment for those who venture into the field is a *machete*, a small shovel, hand claw or garden trowel, a strong pair of walking shoes, insect spray, first-aid kit, water, food, and a back pack for all that, and hopefully for bottles too, on the homeward

7 Local rubbish dumps—especially
Victorian ones, if they can be traced—are
a good source of old bottles.

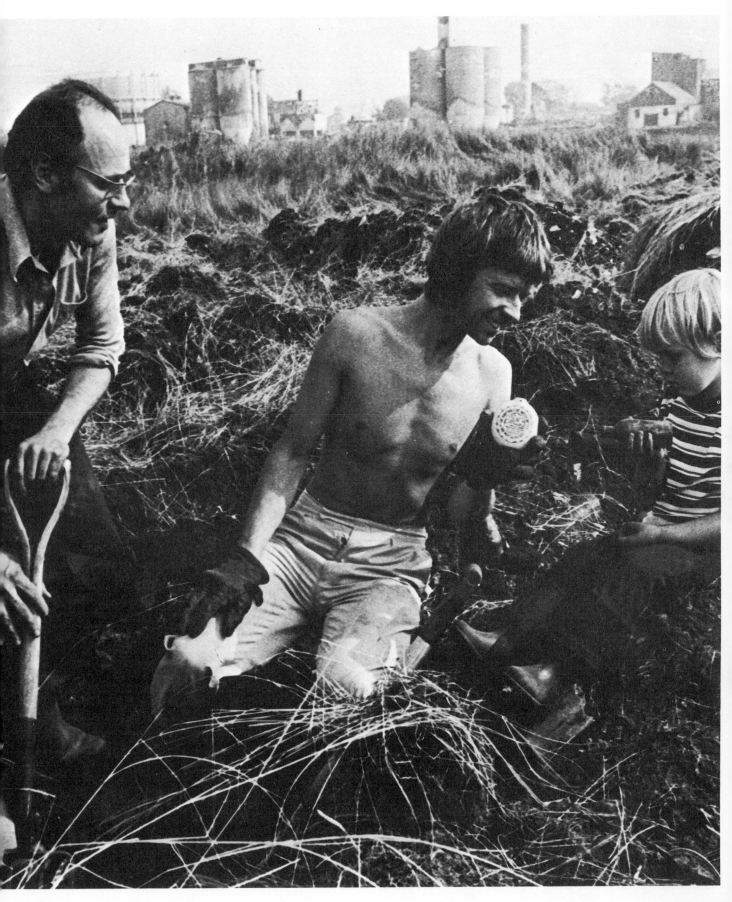

8 An American collection of bottles. The varied shapes and colours look well displayed against a window. (Charles Gardner Collection).

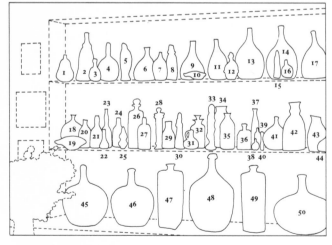

1 Scrolled violin flask
2 Bell-shaped dispensing bottle, marked 'S.M. & Co.'
3 Harden's fire extinguisher
4 Small aqua demijohn
5 Fish bitter bottle
6 New England-type demijohn
7 Red amber reversed tree flask
8 Deep green pickle bottle
9 Deep aqua chestnut bottle
10 Souvenir pig bottle
11 New England-type chestnut bottle
12 Harden's green hand-grenade fire extinguisher
13 Deep aqua chestnut bottle
14 New England-type chestnut bottle
15 Green Bunker Hill cologne
16 Deer and boar canteen flask

17 Deep aqua chestnut bottle
18 S. Wolf & Co. dispensing bottle
19 Pig, marked 'Suffolk Bitters'
20 Union and clasped hands flask
21 Keene square decanter
22 Early Dutch bottle
23 Blue Sazarac bitters
24 Log cabin. Old Homestead bitters
25 Henry Ward Beecher cologne
26 New England jar with witch ball
27 Pikes Peak flask, 'E. Kauffeld'
28 Cannon-shaped General Scott's artillery bitters
29 Blown jar, Pitkin factory
30 Skilton Foote Bunker Hill pickle bottle
31 Handled jug, marked 'W & Co.'
32 Blue drug jar
33 Frosted Indian brave bottle
34 New England-type blown jar

35 New England-type blown jar
36 Original E. G. Booz's Old Cabin Whiskey
37 National Bitters Ear Corn
38 Miniature chestnut bottle
39 Bunker Hill Monument cologne
40 Blue cylindrical cologne
41 Globular New England demijohn
42 Amber Willington pickle bottle with Gothic arch decoration
43 New England blown jar
44 Early kidney-shaped demijohn
45 New England red amber demijohn
46 New England light amber demijohn
47 Square gin or spirit bottle
48 New England-type demijohn
49 Square gin or spirit bottle
50 New England-type demijohn

14

9 Soda-water, gin, beer, wine, poison—
such a variety of shapes makes even a
small collection fascinating. (Mary
Lindsay Collection).

10 Hamilton bowlers, Codd marble
stoppers and stone ginger beer bottles fit
in well with the 'olde worlde' *décor* of a
country pub.

journey. There are some gadgets on the market for bottle-hunters, but they do not seem necessary to get started. Many a fisherman and hunters of a different sort are keeping their eyes open for old bottles nowadays.

There are a few dangers the bottle-hunter should be aware of. Before rushing off to Panama, be warned that you might catch Mud Fever or Weil's Disease there. If you do not slope the sides of a search hole, it might cave in on you as it did on a whole family recently. If you did not get the landowner's permission to dig in the first place, you could also be in trouble with the law! Watch out for snakes, too, and be careful when cleaning old bottles. There can be poison—lead or mercury—in the fumes created by boiling them, for example. A man in Louisiana reportedly died from inhaling such fumes. Ammonia and chlorine bleaches should be avoided at all costs, the simplest and safest way being to soak your finds in cold water to get rid of loose residue and then to give them a second soak in a mild detergent. The greatest hazard for your treasures, once on display, is a rapid change of temperature. Butterfingers should not be allowed to touch!

Natural catastrophes are another matter. The earthquake in southern California in 1971 shattered many a collection, although some bottles were apparently saved by being stuck to their shelves against just such an eventuality. In June 1972, the flood waters of Hurricane Agnes swept into the Glass Museum at Corning in upper New York State, causing untold damage.

8 What was actually contained in many of the bottles now proudly displayed is often still a matter of conjecture. Those marked in some way with their contents are in the minority. Traditional divisions have been made, however, on the basis of surviving evidence and by a process of rationalisation. It is unlikely that anyone but a demonic alchemist would put poison in a quart bottle associated with wine, for example. But more on that later.

It has been estimated that something like two dozen categories of bottles are presently being collected, but when you get right down to it, there are really only two types, not two dozen. They are the alcoholics and the hypochondriacs—metaphorically speaking, of course. But even they overlap, in contents though not always in bottle shape, since the principal ingredient in many medicines until the twentieth century was alcohol. Mineral and soda-water bottles have necks in both camps so to speak: in shape they follow some of the alcoholics, in contents they cater to the hypo-

chondriacs—at least they did until the twentieth century again. Even the highly decorative members of the family—decanters, scent, perfume, toilet bottles, and Chinese snuff bottles—contain stimulants and/or sedatives, depending on need. Perfumes were, after all, used to ward off the noisome odours of the world for hundreds of years before human and environmental cleanliness was devised, to say nothing of their use in the cause of seduction.

A third category presently being collected is something a grab-bag of all other household bottles: those that once held milk, condiments, preserves, honey, snuff, and ink in large quantities, or desk size in the case of ink, shoe blacking, glue and poison.

The oldest known glass bottles, which come from Ancient Egypt and Mesopotamia, once held cosmetics and medicines. Just when alcoholic beverages were first transported in glass bottles is not certain; probably not widely, if at all, before Roman times. 'Bottl'd liquor dealers' were specialised merchants who did not appear on the scene until the nineteenth century. Other commodities went into glass at different times, but none on a large scale until the latter part of the nineteenth century.

But what matter the contents for the moment: just look at those shapes. There are chestnuts and gourds, acorns and sea-nymphs, violins and log cabins, bellows and ears of corn—in fact, practically any animal, mineral or vegetable shape you can think of. There are squats and globs and nips and skinny vials, long necks, short necks, thin necks, thick necks and twisted necks. There are tight-waisted and pinched bottles, expansive and blousy bottles. There is even something called a witch ball. They were once used to ward off evil spirits and at a later date as stoppers for jars and as floaters for fishermen's nets.

And although bottles are not generally highly decorated objects, some have ribs, some stripes, some amethyst streaks or multi-coloured splashes. Others have sunburst patterns embossed back and front, or frilly chains and crimped ribbons of glass trailing around them, or diamonds and stars moulded into their sides. Even simple pickle bottles are moulded with Gothic arches, and a milk bottle has on its side a Quaker milking a cow.

The natural colour range of glass as a result of the oxides in sand and potash or wood ashes is from light green to a brownish amber, and most older bottles are found in that range, greens and greenish blues, called aquamarine, being most common, which is why bottle glass is also called green glass. Unusual colours are

11 Decanter and stopper, favrile glass. Marked L.C.T. for Louis Comfort Tiffany, 1902. Favrile was the name invented by Tiffany for his glass, from the Latin *faber*, meaning a smith. His iridescent and freely shaped glass enjoyed popularity between 1890 and 1915. (Victoria and Albert Museum, London).

12 Bohemian decanter and stopper, *c.* 1840. This is ruby glass, made by the addition of gold, a technique perfected in Germany in the seventeenth century. (Victoria and Albert Museum, London).

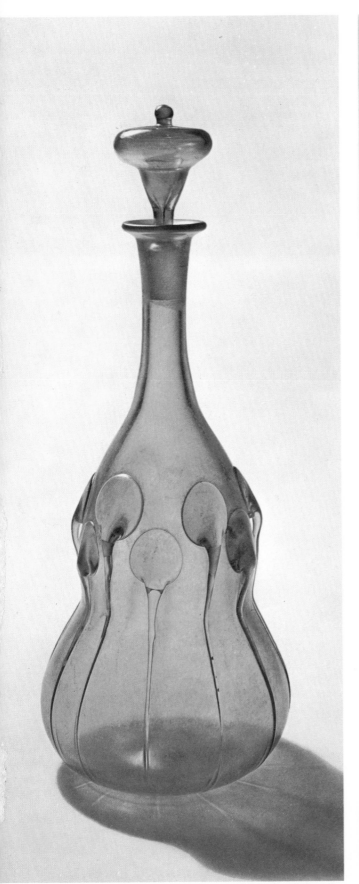

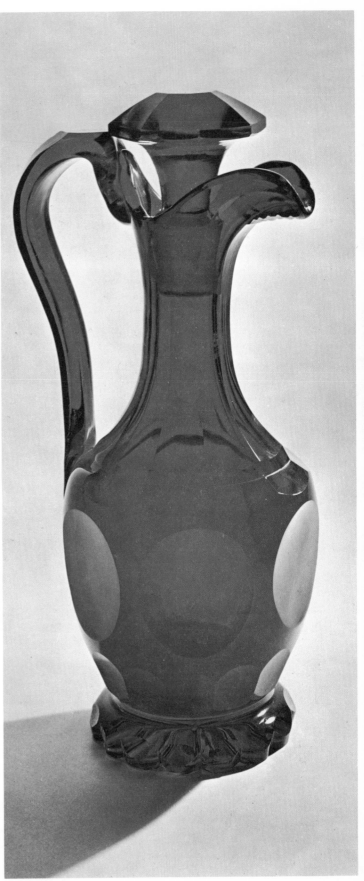

rare in bottles and consequently much sought after by collectors. Layers of colour can be applied to bottles by flashing and staining–dipping them in colour or painting on a colour stain and then firing it in place. There is some indication that both methods have been used to persuade collectors to buy otherwise plain, clear bottles. A little scratch would reveal the awful truth, since the layers of colour can be flaked off. Nature can play its own little tricks with colours, however. The direct, ultra-violet rays of the sun will turn bottles made clear by the addition of manganese and selenium to purples and ambers respectively. The same trick can be achieved with a little help from an ultra-violet lamp. Consult your local physicist!

13 Almost from the time of its discovery, glass has looked like something else. It started out thick and opaque, almost like stone or pottery. The Egyptians in addition wanted it to look like lapis lazuli. The Chinese and early European glass-makers searched for the look of jade, emerald, agate, and other precious and semi-precious stones. Medieval alchemists were set the task of converting the glass into the precious stones, but there is no record that they ever succeeded. Later European glass-makers tried to imitate the porcelains of China or searched for 'a new sort of crystalline glass resembling rock-crystal'–a type of quartz used for ornamental purposes since early times. The so-called art glass of the late nineteenth century was often made in imitation of other materials, such as tortoise-shell. All these searches did not leave bottles untouched.

On one famous occasion the imitating process was reversed. An emperor of the Ch'ing Dynasty in eighteenth-century China took such a liking to the soft colouring of the enamelled glassware produced by Ku Yueh Hsuan that he expressed the wish that porcelain be made to achieve the same effect, and, of course, his wish was granted.

Who actually discovered that a dash of gold would turn a batch of glass first clear and only on re-heating red or ruby coloured remains lost in the misty past. The whole process obviously required a special knack, **12** because after Johann Kunckel, a German chemist working in Potsdam towards the end of the seven-

teenth century, had successfully produced ruby glass on a commercial scale, the art was lost and only re-discovered in the nineteenth century. At that time, English glass-makers were known to appear ceremoniously in their top hats and throw gold sovereigns into the crucible when a batch was being prepared for red glass. It is thought unlikely that the metallic gold would have dispersed in the molten glass–a solution of gold is what is required–so the charming ritual seems to have been connected with the mystic power of gold felt since at least medieval times. It was meant to make the glass brighter or bring good luck, or as one expert has put it, merely demonstrated a well-known tendency of glass-makers in times of trouble to try anything, however unreasonable. The legendary story that Amberina glass was accidentally discovered when a gold ring fell into the batch probably sprang from similar beliefs. Amberina, which shades from a pale straw yellow at the base of a piece to a deep warm ruby **14** at the top, was first made at the works of the New England Glass Company near Boston in the 1880s.

One of the intriguing things about old bottles is that they are sometimes found in a strangely ruined state. Most of us think of glass as being impervious to attack from such corroding agents as acid–which happens to be correct. But glass has another enemy–water–which slowly but surely leaches out the soda and lime –two of the main ingredients in glass–and leaves behind a skeleton of silica or sand which is the principal ingredient. The iridescent colours created by the **16** play of light on this so-called sick glass are sometimes startlingly beautiful. Art Nouveau artists of the late nineteenth century tried to imitate them, and the makers of Carnival glass followed suit. Not many bottles, however, were made in either of these two types of glass. Nature, it has been said, does not need Louis Comfort Tiffany to create its iridescent bottles. In a less advanced stage the corrosion appears as a stain and can be removed.

Other damaged bottles that sometimes charm a collector are those that have become mis-shapen in some unusual way, by the heat from a burning rubbish dump, for example, or whose surfaces have been smoothed away by constant abrasion from sand.

14 A pattern-moulded amberina glass bottle of bipartite glass from the New England Glass Company. 1883 to 1888. (Corning Museum of Glass, New York).

15 Mineral water and beer bottles, 1870 to 1950, on display in the Bell Inn, Finedon, Northamptonshire.

16 Two examples of bottles which have been affected by long periods in the ground. A 'sick' nineteenth-century bullet stopper lemonade bottle and an identical bottle with a rainbow-coloured deposit inside and outside. (Roy Morgan Collection).

17 A Venetian bottle of the seventeenth century, made of dark blue glass with splashes of aventurine glass, in which copper particles remain as glistening flakes. (Victoria and Albert Museum, London).

The history of glass

18 Purple lead-glass bottle by George Ravenscroft, 1675 to 1680. Ravenscroft's experiments with lead oxide as a flux resulted in a solid and heavy glass, more durable than the Venetian glass which it progressively replaced. (Victoria and Albert Museum, London).

making

Before going any further, it might be useful to pause a moment and take a look at some of the highlights in the glass-making story, only sketchily touched on out of context thus far.

As far as we know hollow glass vessels were first made about 1500 BC in ancient Egypt and Mesopotamia. It is impossible to say which, if either, came first. The Roman historian, Pliny, attributed the discovery of glass-making with absolute certainty to the Phoenicians, whose land was roughly what is now the coastal areas of Syria, Lebanon and Israel. The earliest recipes for glass-making known today, however, come from Mesopotamia, but whether they got them from the Egyptians, or the other way round, is still a puzzle.

The ancient Greeks – those giants of early Western culture – do not seem to have gone in for glass-making in the grand manner. At least, no ancient writer found any local industry worthy of mention. There is evidence, though, that ordinary bottles were made in various parts of ancient Greece and recent excavations at Corinth indicate that glass was made there. And even if it turns out to have been no more than ordinary bottles – in the manner in which most writers have of phrasing these things – today's bottle enthusiasts might raise a ragged cheer.

The old Romans knew a good thing when they heard about it, and they soon had a flourishing industry spreading into the furthest corners of their vast empire – the fancy stuff as well as ordinary household bottles – and glassware was no longer a luxury only available to the aristocratic levels of society. There is some evidence that glass-making was carried on in Britain during the Roman occupation, but it is not certain whether the Roman bottles that have been unearthed there were actually produced locally or imported from some other part of the Roman Empire.

The decline in Roman power brought a corresponding decline in glass-making throughout the lands once ruled by Rome. But thanks to the bottle-makers who took refuge in small, isolated forest glass-houses, the art of glass-making did not entirely die out.

Like many another chemical art, high-style glass-making had its first re-birth after the decline of Roman power in the area where it was born – the Middle East, and more specifically in the countries converted to Islam – Egypt, Syria, Mesopotamia, Persia. And it was in that area where from about the ninth to the four-teenth centuries richly gilded, enamelled and intricately patterned glass was particularly outstanding.

21

23

19 Lustre glass bottle made by the firm
of J. Lötz Witwe, Klostermühle, Bohemia.
This was shown at the Paris Exhibition
of 1900. (Victoria and Albert Museum,
London).

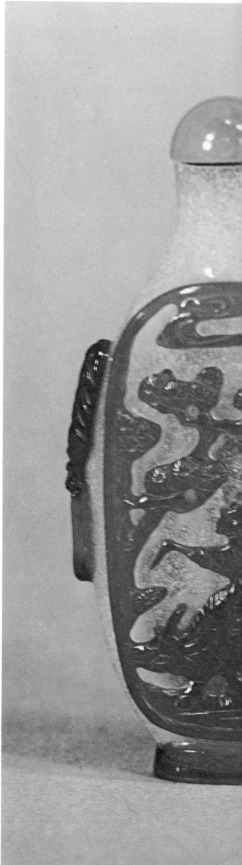

20 Chinese snuff bottles of the Ch'ing Dynasty, eighteenth to nineteenth century. Opaque white glass with a green cameo of a gourd with a vine, and white camphor with a red cameo of a man and an ox under a pine tree. (Seattle Art Museum, Washington).

A Persian sprinkler bottle of the
twelfth century AD. It is mould-blown in
pale green glass and the design is related
to the earthenware of the time. (Pilkington
Glass Museum, St Helens, Lancashire).

and from Byzantium to the North may have moved to Venice and helped establish an industry there which from the fifteenth to the seventeenth centuries produced glassware that was the envy of all Europe. Venetian craftsmen re-discovered the art of making clear glass, although a greyish tone is sometimes noted in their finest *cristallo*, and excelled in airy-fairy fantasies devised from molten glass in rich tones of purples, blues and greens as well as clear glass. But the range of their skills seems to have been limitless.

17

The Venetians were tyrannical masters and did their best to keep their craftsmen and their secrets under lock and key on the island of Murano. But many of them were spirited away to set up shop in other parts of Europe, notably France, Spain and the Netherlands. Consequently Venetian-type glass might have been made in any of the many places to which Venetian craftsmen, or others trained by them, took their skills, even in the faraway Puebla de los Angeles, near which the Spanish conquerors of what is now Mexico reported a glass-making industry was flourishing by about 1542.

Meanwhile, back in the hinterlands of Europe, the old bottle-makers had been plodding away at their mundane task, and a few of the more adventurous ones, when they were not copying Venetian work, tried out something different. They began using the talents of other craftsmen to decorate their wares – or maybe it was the other way around. In any event, copper wheel engraving, a jeweller's craft, was re-discovered in Prague as a means of decorating glass towards the end of the seventeenth century, and was subsequently followed throughout Bohemia and Germany, and as far away as what is now the Netherlands and Belgium. Much of the glass decorated in this way consequently has to be designated Bohemian or German, German or Dutch, or simply Central European. In Antwerp, in particular, craftsmen also gave distinction to diamond-point engraving on glass.

Towards the end of the seventeenth century the action shifted to England, where in 1674 George Ravenscroft patented his method for making lead glass, a new way of obtaining clear or crystal glass. And for much of the eighteenth century everyone was imitating the English style. Lead glass is softer than the soda-lime variety used in Venice – and therefore lends itself more easily to cutting – a decorative technique for which English and Irish houses became well known. Even today, lead crystal,

18

as it is more grandly referred to, is much vaunted by manufacturers in a number of countries. So-called Nailsea glass, named after its assumed production at factories in that town near Bristol, England, but made in many others including those at Alloa in Scotland, is characterised by stripes and splashes in white enamel mostly on smoky-green to brown bottle glass. It is not unlike what is called *latticino* decoration in Italian ware. The Bristol factories are also famous for their opaque white, dark blue and green glass, as well as bottle production.

Just about the time when English glass-making was being put on the map, Chinese glass-makers were cleverly imitating the texture of such precious materials as jade, emerald and the porcelains for which they were justly renowned. In the eighteenth century, in particular, snuff bottles get special mention. Glass-making was known in both China and Japan around the turn of the centuries from BC to AD.

20

The glass-making art seems to have spread to India from Persia and became notable in that country for the rich gold decoration, inspired by miniature painting, in the seventeenth century.

On the basis of surviving evidence the French remained in the 'bottles only' class at least until the nineteenth century, when special mention has to be made of the work of Emile Gallé in particular. The stained glass window artists of the twelfth and thirteenth centuries were specialists who did not concern themselves with any other type of glass-making. Many French glass-makers are known to have crossed the Channel into England in medieval times, however, and played a significant role in the re-establishment of glass-making there.

As mentioned above, glass-making in what became the United States of America was also in the 'mainly bottles' class (which includes window glass) until the nineteenth century. Some of those bottles, as we shall see, were very pretty. In the nineteenth century the new Republic contributed to the technical innovations that were revolutionising the production of glassware, and in 1903 Michael Owens perfected the first fully automatic bottle-making machine. At about the same time the original and individualistic tableware of Louis Comfort Tiffany was receiving world-wide acclaim.

In the twentieth century the work of Austrian and Swedish glass-makers is usually singled out as being particularly outstanding.

19

22 Embossments could identify the store selling the bottle (left), or assist in usage showing graduations for a medicine bottle (right).

How to make a bottle

The ingredients of glass have altered little since humans first started cooking it up thousands of years ago. If you mix a lot of sand with a little soda and lime **24** in a large crucible and heat it to something like 2500°F., you will have molten glass. There are a few other ingredients but they need not concern us here. In medieval Europe, potash or wood ashes obtained from burning wood or bracken largely replaced soda which was less available than it was in the Middle East. Oil, gas or electricity have replaced coal and wood as the principal fuel in getting up that heat, and considerably less fuel is required to do it than in the days when forests were being torn down at an alarming rate to feed the furnaces. A little glass-making occurs without human intervention when lightning strikes sand, or when volcanic action gets to it. The result is long slender tubes called fulgurites and a dark vitreous lava or volcanic rock known as obsidian.

If you want to play around with the colours you would get naturally–the greens and browns mentioned above–you would throw in a few drops of metallic oxide as follows:

            copper, selenium, gold for   reds
            nickel or manganese . . . . . . purples
            chromium or copper . . . . . . greens
            cobalt or copper . . . . blues
            carbon or nickel . . . . browns
            iron . . . . greens, yellows
            selenium . . . . yellows, pinks
            tin or zinc . . . . opal or milk-glass
            iron slag . . . . 'black'
            uranium . . . . greenish yellow

Clear glass is obtained in a variety of ways. The Venetians used manganese for their famous *cristallo* and so did the manufacturers of many late nineteenth-century bottles. George Ravenscroft discovered that a healthy dollop of lead produced a brilliantly clear glass. Of course, it is a little confusing the way those oxides sometimes have very differing results: manganese produces purple, clear and black glass, for example, and copper produces reds and blues. It all depends on the original mix, proportions and so on, the tantalising variables which a good cook knows how to handle, but which drive a novice to drink.

But to get back to the molten glass and its shaping and baking. The key to shaping most glass is blowing, either by humans or machines. But we will probably never know which inventive genius figured it out.

The early Egyptians did not blow: they dipped, that is, they made their hollow glass vessels by poking and shaping a blob of molten glass with a clay or sand

23 A scene in a Brooklyn glasshouse—
blowpipes and pontils are much in
evidence.

24 Kempster Mural. As the mountains are eroded, grains of quartz are washed down to form beds of silica sand – the basic ingredient of glass. (Pilkington Glass Museum, St Helens, Lancashire).

core covered in some kind of textile. At least, that is one theory. Another is that softened canes of glass were wound around the core. However, microscopic analysis of surviving examples, dated roughly 1500 BC, has shown no fine structure of streamers or trains of bubbles which apparently would be present if such a method had been used. Science is still considering the matter.

There is some speculation that blowing down a hollow tube into the blob of molten glass may have come about as the glass-makers made the rods for their cores longer and longer to avoid burning their fingers. It is an interesting possibility, but just how this earth-shaking experiment actually came about remains a matter of speculation, although the evidence points to its having taken place in Syria about 100 BC. It seems to have been an immediate hit.

In the *Talmud* breathing shape and form into molten glass is likened not inappropriately to God's breathing life into the human body. Is it any wonder that glass-blowing is among the ancient crafts that are being revived in certain areas today and is even being used for therapeutic purposes?

'If you wish to make bottles,' said a thirteenth-century expert, 'this do. When you have gathered some hot glass on the end of a blowing tube and blown it in the form of a large bladder, swing the tube with

the glass appended to it, and the neck will be stretched
by this action . . .' You should also remember that
the glass has to stay hot for that action, that is, in a
semi-molten and ductile state during the entire
shaping process. In other words, you have to work fast
or know just when and how much to re-heat. Bottles
were made in just such a fashion until well into the
23 nineteenth century, with occasional help from a few
basic tools. The large carboys and demijohns took a
lot of blowing as you can imagine. Scottish glass-
makers, towards the end of the eighteenth century,
apparently made a speciality of large bottles, sometimes with a capacity of over one hundred gallons!
More than human breath was needed for the expan-
sion of these globular-shaped vessels, however. It
seems that spirit was poured in after the initial blowing
25 and 'the force generated by the vapourised alcohol
was sufficient to expand the bulb to the required
capacity'.

The minor quirks in shape—the slightly asymmetrical contours or off-centre neck, particularly on
the large bottles—are some of the charms of free-
blown bottles. Making consistent or precise measure-
ments was obviously not an easy task, and only the
later, more widespread use of full-size moulds and

mechanised production brought about the standard-
isation we know today.

Many of the shapes mentioned earlier, however,
were created in whole or in part by the use of moulds,
at first in combination with human blowing and later
with mechanical blowing and pressing.

The earliest type of dip mould was simply used to
form the body of a bottle—the remainder from the
shoulder up being completed by hand methods. It is
sometimes, though by no means always, possible
to see a seam mark where the blow-over—as the glass
used to form the shoulder and lip is called—is joined
to the body section. The seams left by piece moulds—
pieces or leaves hinged together in various ways—are
more noticeable and are being used nowadays as a
rough guide in dating bottles. Bottles were mould-
blown as early as the seventeenth and eighteenth
centuries in Europe, but not often in America before
the nineteenth century.

Variations on the basic moulds are called pattern
moulds and are used to emboss a wide variety of
designs on to the glass. A mould with perpendicular
ridges gives a ribbed effect to a bottle, which can be
swirled to right or left with a little deft manipulation
after the bottle is removed from the mould. A little

26 Moulds with several hinged pieces left lines on the bottle where the pieces joined and if these lines remain, they indicate what type of mould was used. The simplest mould was a dip mould, merely a container into which the glass vessel was blown. A pattern mould with ribs inside was used in the making of the bottles with a ribbed or swirled design.

27 Stiegel flasks, diamond and daisy, diamond and rib and diamond designs blown from a pattern mould.

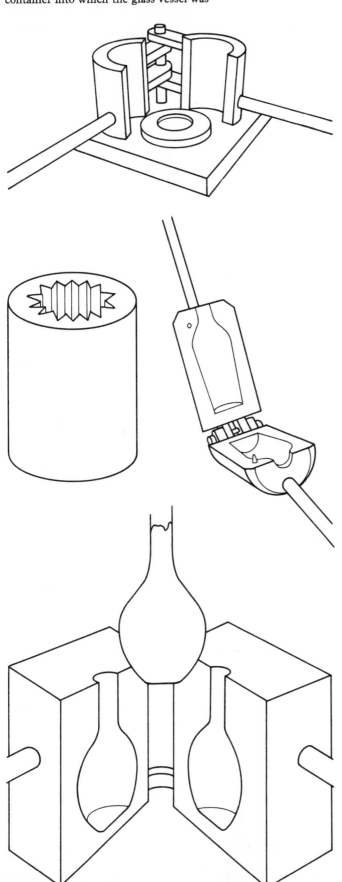

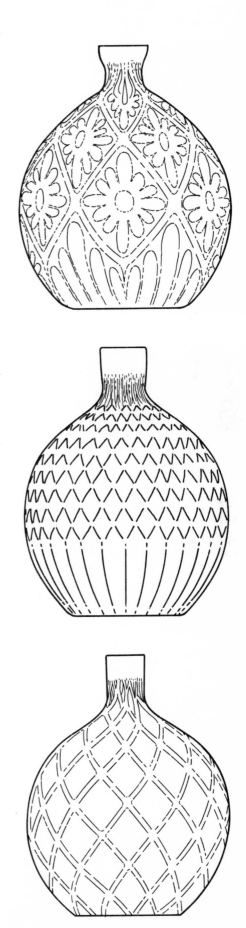

28 A Stiegel flask with a swirled rib design. (Cincinnatti Art Museum, Ohio).

29 Blue glass scent bottle, cut, gilt and enamelled. Bristol, eighteenth century. (Schreiber Collection. Victoria and Albert Museum, London).

30 Diagram of fully automatic blow-and-blow process for making bottles.

28   **29**

30

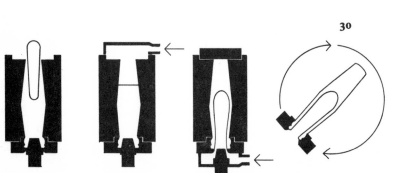
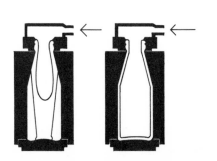

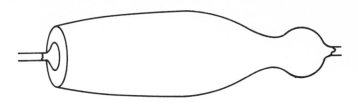

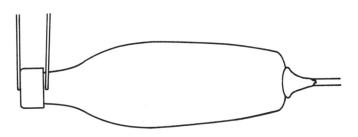

31 When a vessel has been blown, it must be held at the base by a pontil before it can be removed from the blow pipe.

more blowing will expand the pattern in interesting ways, and a second and even a third dip in the same mould or a different one can be used to double up the pattern or criss-cross it. Diamonds and diamonds

27 with daisies in them are only a few of the many designs moulded on to bottles and expanded. A whole gamut of folk art emblems and scenes in flat relief were created by the full-size moulds used for the much prized American whisky flasks of the first part of the nineteenth century. And since they were used time and time again, it is thought that these latter moulds must have been made of metal, which would have been the only way of getting a sharply defined outline each time. Simpler moulds were probably made of clay or wood.

More mundane things like a manufacturer's name or the bottle's contents are also embossed on the sides or bases of bottles from moulds, and are often highly

22 valued by collectors.

Mould embossing is, in fact, the principal method of decorating bottles, although all the sophisticated techniques developed for fine glass (cutting, engraving, etching, gilding, enamelling and overlaying) can be found on the rare bottle, but usually among the

29 fancier forms such as decanters, perfume, toilet water and snuff bottles. The same is true of the more elaborate moulded designs such as the geometric, Baroque and architectural or arch patterns blown principally in three-part moulds during the early part of the nineteenth century and the fanciful Rococo designs of pressed glass later in the century. Both types are early examples of mass-production. One authority has listed more than three hundred popular designs in pressed glass. One of the easiest differences to remember between these two types of moulded glass is that vessels made by a mechanical plunger, pressing the glass into the moulds, have smooth interiors, whereas those shaped and decorated by human blowing into the mould have the pattern formed on the outside of the vessel reversed on the inside. This latter type of glass has a number of misleading names. The most accurate and illuminating that I have seen is three-part mould-blown ware. Seams are visible on most vessels made in this manner, but were made to vanish by fire polishing on the pressed ware.

Controversy still rages over what exactly causes 'whittle' marks. It used to be thought that the crude, wavy, dimpled or hammered appearance found on the surface of some bottles had been caused by wooden moulds—hence the name whittle marks. Then it was discovered that such marks could also

have been caused when hot glass was blown into cold moulds at the beginning of the day's work. That theory now seems to hold sway over most collectors. But two others have been put forward explaining the marks as the result of non-vented moulds, or of the marks on iron moulds cast from wooden models. It does not look as though the issue is going to be settled any time soon.

Once the bottle had life and shape and decoration, the problem was to get it off the blow-pipe. This was partially solved by attaching another rod or pipe to the bottom of the vessel. Then a slap from a wet **31** stick 'melted' the bottle away from the blow-pipe at the neck. The holding process is known as empontilling, the holder a pontil (pronounce the 'l'). The names puntellium, punte, pontie and punty are dropping out of use. The mark left by the pontil after it is broken off is a rough scar. Its presence indicates that the vessel was probably made prior to the middle of the nineteenth century. After about that time the holding process was done by what is called a snap—a kind of four-pronged harpoon which formed a cradle into which the bottle was placed for the neck-finishing process. When the pontil was pushed up into the base of the bottle before being broken off, it formed what is called a kick-up.

The final baking is the reverse of what happens in the kitchen: the finished vessel goes into an annealing oven, so that it can be cooled off gradually and in that way harden and strengthen into glass as we know it.

By the end of the nineteenth century, bottle-making had been mechanised in a variety of ways, and today the entire process is done by machines: the gathering of the initial gob of molten glass, either by suction or a mechanical feeding device, the shaping of neck and body—in machine production the neck is formed before the body, just the reverse of what happens with hand methods—and final dispatch to the annealing ovens.

The bottles themselves

wine bottles

The earliest glass vessels known today that might have contained wine are those found in the Middle East and throughout the areas of Europe once ruled by Rome between about the first century BC and the fifth century AD. We even know the names of some of the glass-makers. Frontinus, a glass-maker in Picardy, France, for example, has his name inscribed on a number of barrel-shaped bottles which might have **34** been used for the local wine trade. One such can be seen in the Victoria and Albert Museum in London. But any of the numerous shapes which have survived from that early period might have contained wine, particularly those shaped like bunches of grapes, and those portraying Bacchus and other Gods of Revelry.

After the disintegration of the Roman Empire, wine seems to have gone back into leather, earthenware and stoneware bottles, and stayed there, or rather went on being put there almost until the seventeenth century. In that long interval, it seems that the only glass bottles being made in the greater part of Europe were used primarily for medicines. Bottles of Persian and Syrian origin roughly dated between about the seventh and fourteenth centuries, during the ascendancy of Mohammedan princes in that area, almost certainly contained some type of beverage.

Small hexagonal and octagonal shaped bottles, mostly made of a dark brown glass and roughly dated between the fourth and sixth centuries AD, have been found in the Middle East and are called Pilgrim bottles. They are thought to have been ritual vessels used to contain holy oil and are noticeably similar, whether the symbols moulded on their sides are Jewish or Christian.

Italian paintings of the late fifteenth century show that wine was back in rather elegant glass serving-bottles, but there is little evidence that they were in widespread use elsewhere in Europe.

By the end of the seventeenth century, however, Britain was producing practically all the bottles she needed, and had thereby 'quite spoiled' the import business from Sweden, in the words of one satisfied observer. The pioneers of a local industry in America in the late eighteenth and early nineteenth centuries urged their friends and neighbours to a similar patriotic independence of British imports.

The principal shape of the seventeenth-century British bottle is a fat globular body, which initially

33 Three distinct shapes all for wine. Left to right: Burgundy, Claret and Hock. These shapes had evolved in the various wine-growing districts abroad and began to appear in England after 1802.

34 A small Roman bottle made in the third or fourth century AD. On the underside is a moulded inscription FRON –short for Frontinus. (Pilkington Glass Museum, St Helens, Lancashire).

had a very long neck, but since that proved very **35** unstable, it was soon replaced by a shorter one. The long neck version is sometimes referred to as a shaft and globe.

Wine bottles were certainly being made in the eastern United States as early as the seventeenth century, but it is generally thought that those that have survived from that period were probably imported either from Britain or Holland.

By the early part of the eighteenth century the sides of bottles began to settle down into straighter lines–there were minor variations in the curves at shoulder and base in the second half of the seventeenth century–and from then on they began to grow taller and thinner by the decade. The narrow, cylindrical shape of the average wine bottle of today is known in a **33** slightly asymmetrical, free-blown form as early as 1737. The more standard moulded versions appeared in the latter part of the eighteenth century. There were not a few variations around the basic line of development and many shapes probably co-existed quite happily for years. Some of the squats and globs, as they are rather graphically labelled, were more egg-shaped or kidney-shaped than others. Dutch bottles of the late seventeenth and early eighteenth centuries are said to have longer necks on average and a higher kick-up. A particularly high kick-up is called an Indian bottle in America, in memory of the deceptive trading practices that went on in those raw early days of exploration and acquisition. The late eighteenth-century French wine bottle had a body more like a flower-pot, a shape given by Denis Diderot in his famous Encyclopedia published between 1751 and 1780.

An interesting find of French bottles was made in the U.S.S.R. a few years ago. They might conceivably have been buried by one of Napoleon's commissaries during the retreat the Emperor had to make from Moscow in the winter of 1812.

Octagonal-sided wine bottles are also found in America, but are rare in Britain in the eighteenth century–evidence that the colonists readily defied the mother country's edict about only importing from Britain, or simply of the German roots of their pioneer glass-makers.

More decorative bottles of the eighteenth century with flattened oval or rounded bodies and a variety of pattern-moulded designs, which might have contained wine, are more often thought of as flasks which were used for spirits–whisky, brandy or rum, perhaps–and will be dealt with under that heading.

35 A typical globular shaped bottle made in England or Spain in the early eighteenth century. (Victoria and Albert Museum, London).

36 Seals used to identify bottles belonging to the White Bear Tavern, London, and to Dean Swift. (Charles Gardner Collection).

Plain olive green and amber globular-shaped bottles with longish necks are sometimes called Ludlows in the United States of America, but were certainly made over a long period in other factories besides that at Ludlow, Massachusetts, from which they take their name.

The average capacity of wine bottles ranges from about a pint, to something like a gallon. The larger bottles in the 1- to 10-gallon range, and sometimes larger, are called demijohns and carboys. The Middle East is often said to have been the source of both words. There is no dispute as far as carboy is concerned. It seems to be accepted as a mild corruption of a Persian word *qar(r)abah*. It is a different story with demijohn. The earliest source seems to be a seventeenth-century French word, *dame-jeanne*, from which everyone else borrowed it, even the Persians and the Arabs.

The carboy is the larger of the two, generally in the 6- to 10-gallon range, and usually thicker, since it seems to have been the prime means of transporting acids and other corrosive chemicals, as well as wine and rosewater. Both retained the bulbous, globular shapes of the seventeenth century, even after the smaller sizes developed straight sides. I do not know of any special name given to the enormous, 100-gallon and more capacity of the bottles the Scots specialised in, as mentioned earlier. Roughly half that quantity would have been a hogshead.

The most common colour for all wine bottles, until well into the nineteenth century, was a very dark green or brown, sometimes called black. The larger demijohns and carboys are sometimes found in a clear glass. Bottles from the later nineteenth century have a wider range of colours, and some of these with either unusual colours or embossments are beginning to attract the collector's interest.

Since wine bottles were constantly re-used – that is, taken to the local tavern or merchant for a re-fill – it
37 was common practice for aristocratic customers to have seals bearing their coat-of-arms, initials or other mark of identity applied to the shoulder or body of the bottle on blobs of glass. Tavern owners, merchants,
36 distillers and shipping agents often followed suit. Such notables as cleric and author, Jonathan Swift, and the carpenter from Philadelphia, William Savery, also had their seals placed on bottles, examples of which are known. The seals often had a date on them, and that has been the principal means of determining the changes that took place in wine bottle shapes from about 1650 to the mid nineteenth century. The

37 Taverns, clubs and wealthier private people had their bottles made with an embossed glass seal on the shoulder. These seals usually bore the name, initials or crest of the owner. In this group are seals with dukes' and barons' coronets, a bishop's mitre, a comet—perhaps to commemorate the appearance of a comet. The undergraduates of St John's College had a seal which was distinct from that of the dons—St I.C.R. for St John's Common Room. The last three seals are American, eighteenth century.

38 The earliest known wine bottle with a seal, owned by the King's Head, probably in Oxford. (Central Museum, Northampton).

39 Ale bottles by E. and J. Burke in 1886.
This is the oldest full bottle in the
Guinness Museum, Dublin.

earliest seal–without its bottle–was supposed to be
dated 1562, but it seems to have disappeared, as does
the first bottle once known with a seal dated 1652.
Consequently the earliest wine bottle with a dated seal
known today is one in the Central Museum in Northampton, England. The date is 1657 and the owner
38 seems to have been the King's Head Tavern, probably
in nearby Oxford. One of the eighteenth-century
bottles owned by the American collector, Charles
Gardner of Connecticut, bears the seal of what is
thought to have been a tavern once situated hard by
old London Bridge.

Many bottles nowadays thought to have contained
wine undoubtedly contained other liquids–oil and
honey perhaps during Roman times, mineral water,
probably from the time of its popularity in Europe
as early as the seventeenth century, vinegar, and
certainly spirits including liqueurs, and cider and
beer, which were widely consumed, but for only some
of which distinctive shapes gradually developed.
Joseph Crellins, a glass-maker of Quincy, Massachusetts, supposedly specialised in cider bottles for
export to the West Indies about the middle of the
eighteenth century, but they do not seem to have
differed noticeably from the wine bottles of the time.

beer bottles

As with wine, in Britain at least, beer was probably
put into glass bottles for the first time sometime
41 during the seventeenth century. But since both the
drink and the glass bottle were taxed by the Crown, it
is thought unlikely that much bottling was done except
for the rich, at least until the repeal of the tax on glass
about the middle of the nineteenth century.

A Virginia merchant sent a request to a London sea
captain in 1759 for '50 groce of cheap corks for small
beer', and went on, 'in case you go to any place where
bottles are cheap buy me 4 groce'. The 'small beer'
were probably smaller versions of the more or less
straight sided, squat wine bottles of the time. They
may not have been made of glass. I cannot tell if or
where the captain found cheap bottles.

Pale and expensive ales from such brewing towns
as Nottingham, Derby and Burton-on-Trent in
England were remarked upon in highly favourable

40 A collection of nineteenth-century beer bottles. (Mary Lindsay Collection).

41 The evolution of the beer bottle from the eighteenth century to the present day. The straight-sided bottles made storage easier.

ASHBY'S AUSTRALIAN PALE ALE.

THIS ALE, which has for many years been shipped to the Australian markets, where it is in high repute, resembles in those properties for which it is so strongly recommended by the faculty, the East India Pale Ales; but being brewed for a climate of lower temperature, and possessing a finer flavour and greater body, it will be found more congenial to the British taste. The attention of families is especially invited to this Ale, as it is particularly adapted to private use. It may be had, and bottled in excellent condition, in casks of 9 and 18 gallons, as received from the Brewery, at Staines; of Wm. Hancock, 83, Connaught-terrace, London Agent. Orders by post (free) punctually attended to.

tones by the London literati of the latter part of the seventeenth century, and are usually priced per dozen bottles, rather than by the cask, in household records of the period. But contemporary comment on any peculiarities of the bottles themselves seems to be lacking. The quantities appear to have been relatively insignificant, and it is generally assumed that they must have been the same as those used for wine. They may not have been glass.

Porter, on the other hand, the stronger, darker beer, first brewed in London about 1720 and lasting in public favour until about 1830, is associated with a particular type of bottle which is very like the wine shape of the latter part of the eighteenth century. The name porter was supposedly given to this type of beer because of the liking evinced for it by porters—heavy manual workers of the day.

Early nineteenth-century advertisements in American newspapers for porter bottles show a straight sided bottle with a short, slightly bulging neck. Some look sleeker than others. The not-so-sleek are referred to disparagingly as junk bottles.

The best porter bottles were made in Bristol, England, apparently—at least that was the standard of excellence that the Philadelphia glass-maker, Dr. Thomas W. Dyott, claimed he could match in the 1820s.

By about the 1840s the common small size was about half a pint and appeared in a wide range of colours. But many of the beer bottles presently being collected come from the later 1870–1920 period, by **44** which time a fairly characteristic shape had evolved— the slender cylindrical body with tapering shoulders. Many American collectors like to concentrate on the output of one particular brewery, such as the Eagle Brewery in San Jose, where Old Joe's Steam Beer was produced. Steam beer seems to have been popular in west coast breweries because it was faster to make.

The Guinness Company founded in Dublin in 1759 was by the end of the nineteenth century the largest and most eminent brewery in Europe and

44 Four beer bottles. Left to right: entirely hand-made; machine-made with a hand-applied neck; machine-made bottle with a long neck; crown-sealed bottle. Many attempts had been made to devise more satisfactory closures for beer bottles. In 1872 the internal screw stopper was patented by an Englishman, Henry Barrett, and the crown cork in 1892 by an American, William Painter. (Guinness Museum, Dublin).

remains today the largest industrial enterprise in the Republic of Ireland.

Unusual colours, embossments and paper labels are some of the things that attract collectors to the beer bottles of those years. One particularly intriguing paper label found in America on a cobalt blue bottle carries the inscription 'Liquid Bread—A Pure Extract of Malt'. Liquid bread is of course a literal translation of a type of beer brewed in Southern Germany, *Flüssiges Brot*.

Much interest is also focused on the closures of beer bottles towards the end of the nineteenth century. Home brewers of ale in the early part of the seventeenth century were all too aware of the hazards of using corks. As one expert cautioned, 'be sure that the corks be fast tied in with strong Pack thread, for fear of rising out, and taking vent, which is the utter spoil of the ale'. Numerous efforts were made to devise more satisfactory closures. By the end of the nineteenth century two still known today had been invented: the internal screw stopper patented in 1872 by an Englishman, Henry Barret, and the crown cork or cap invented in 1891 by an American, William Painter.

In 1920, beer along with all other alcoholic beverages was prohibited throughout the United States of America. The last bottles produced before the ban was enforced consequently have a particular historic interest. One such bottle is known to have been insured for $25,000, or something over £10,500. One or two of the more unusual glass bottles used for beer since Prohibition ended in 1933 have recently been attracting collectors' interest and perhaps more will, if tin cans ever succeed in replacing glass bottles entirely as the most common containers for beer.

46

45 A collection of labels for stout sold around 1900. (Guinness Museum, Dublin).

46 The traditional gin bottle assumed this tapering shape in the eighteenth century. The same shape is in use today. (Mary Lindsay Collection).

spirits bottles

Of the distilled liquors usually referred to as spirits—whisky, gin, brandy, rum, vodka and schnapps—only the first two have become associated with distinctive bottle shapes as far as bottle collectors are concerned. The distinctiveness is somewhat arbitrary—brandy, rum, various liqueurs, wine and even cider almost certainly went into similar bottles. Nevertheless, the distinction has become traditional and this is not the moment to flout tradition. Anyone wanting to collect vodka and schnapps bottles will have to do some research on the importing and exporting patterns and/or other people's drinking habits.

Gin—short for geneva, a now unused version of the Dutch for juniper, which is the drink's principal flavouring—was first distilled by a Dutch doctor working in Leyden in the mid seventeenth century. He was searching for a diuretic to promote kidney function at the time and his discovery was, in fact, first used as a medicine. It quickly became so popular that apothecaries switched to full-time gin-distilling. English soldiers campaigning on the Continent supposedly took it home with them, and by the end of the century the English nobility had been introduced to it by the Dutch Prince of Orange, who became their sovereign, William III.

The traditional bottle shape associated with gin from the seventeenth century onwards is a tall, square-based, rectangular one with hunched, almost squared-off shoulders and a short stubby neck. They are known as case bottles, because they were often packed in sets in specially-made wooden cases. The more or less straight sides of the seventeenth-century version began to taper to a narrower base in the eighteenth century. It is almost impossible to distinguish between the Dutch, English or American-made versions of this bottle, or to give anything but a rough date to their manufacture. Seals are rare on bottles of this type and even rarer with dates. Unlike some wines and beers, spirits do not improve in flavour after being bottled. Signs of wear do not really help much because deterioration in glass takes place at very different rates. Crosses, concentric circles and occasionally Arabic figures have been found on smaller eighteenth-century versions partially obscured by pontil marks, but their significance has not yet been established.

Most case bottles are in dark shades of olive and

47 A young man drinking, by Murillo (1617–82). He is holding a case-bottle, so called because it was designed to fit into a wooden case holding a dozen. (National Gallery, London).

olive amber, but they are occasionally found in lighter colours, even in clear glass. At least one example is known in white milk-glass.

Many of these bottles have been coming to light in recent years in and around the Panama Canal. Some of them have a more flattened shape – they are sometimes dubbed coffins – and were probably made in the latter part of the nineteenth century. They may also have been used for whisky or other spirits. A harum-scarum chicken – rooster, perhaps? – tearing along on a penny-farthing bicycle, feathers a-flyin', is one of the unusual embossments found on these later bottles. People, animals, birds, stars and crests, as well as lettering, were commonly embossed on late nineteenth-century bottles and are highly valued by collectors.

Another type of case bottle which might have held spirits, liqueurs or even toilet waters, is thought to be a peculiarly Germanic type. It often has a more oblong base and is frequently decorated front and back with enamels and gilt, simple cutting or engraving. The only chance one would have of obtaining the more elegant of those associated with the names of Henry William Stiegel and Frederick Amelung in America would be to inherit them. The simpler, cruder versions are not particularly sought after. Some are thought to have been used as tea-caddies.

Much work still remains to be done on the peculiarities of any of the bottles used for liqueurs. One in particular, a tall, skinny bottle with a thin cylindrical neck and a narrow, more or less rectangular or cylindrical body which contained Maraschino, a cherry liqueur exported by the Luxardo Company in Italy, is attracting an increasing following in the United States of America. These bottles have been found in California and Colorado gold fields. At least one example is dated as early as 1855. The company was established in Dalmatia in 1821 and re-established in Italy after its factories were destroyed during World War II.

The bottle shapes associated with whisky are much more varied than those associated with gin or other spirits, but they are just as likely to have contained the other life-giving waters – the word whisky is a contraction of the Gaelic words *uisque-beatha* meaning *water of life*. The Latin *aqua vitae* was a common term used by alchemists and others for all spirits. For the French the water of life, *eau-de-vie*, is of course brandy, and for the Scandinavians it is *aquavit*.

Legend has it that St Patrick taught the Irish the art of distilling and that they in turn taught the Scots.

However that may be, distilling was certainly more important than brewing in northern Scotland and Ireland at least until the nineteenth century. Distilleries were apparently set up in England during the reign of Henry VIII by Irish immigrants.

The chances of finding bottles in the illicit stills which flourished in the Highlands of Scotland for a good part of the seventeenth and eighteenth centuries, however, are negligible, since Scotch was not actually sold in bottles until 1846.

Credit for selling the first bottled Scotch is given to John Dewar, founder of the company that sells a blended whisky known throughout the world as 'White Label', when he began business in a small wine and spirit shop in Perth, Scotland. There is some evidence that the first bottles used were made of stoneware rather than glass. In the 1890s a case of Dewar's bottled Scotch was ordered even by the White House.

A black bottle with a neat white label was first used by James Buchanan around the turn of the nineteenth century and the combination actually gave his blend its name, 'Black & White', registered in 1904.

Glass pocket flasks were widely used, of course, along the old coaching routes throughout the British Isles. They seem to have been made of thick glass and decorated with strips and bosses of glass as a protection against breakage. An advertisement in a Newcastle newspaper, late in the eighteenth century stated, 'Stolen in Newcastle one white glass Pocket Bottle, with Barley Corns engraved upon it.' Very flat, stretched-out oval shapes with the swirling white enamel stripes characteristic of Nailsea are also known.

Canadian whisky was apparently first sold in bottles in 1853, and there is a rumour about Australian collectors favouring a Ned Kelly bottle.

Much more is known about the types of bottles used to carry whisky in the United States.

American collectors are particularly attached to four types of whisky flasks made mostly from about 1820 to 1870, but also around the turn of the eighteenth century. All four types – Pitkins, chestnuts, and what are called pictorial and historical flasks – are now mainly in the hands of big private collectors or on display in museums, because they were being collected as early as the 1920s by those with an interest in American-made glass. But they did travel – one was found in a ship sunk off Bermuda some time ago, so there is always the chance that they will turn up in odd places. They are usually thought of as pocket flasks, but probably graced many a table as well.

48 A typical pair of Pitkin flasks with a swirled and fluted pattern. (Charles Gardner Collection).

49 Chestnut flasks with diamond and ribbed patterns.

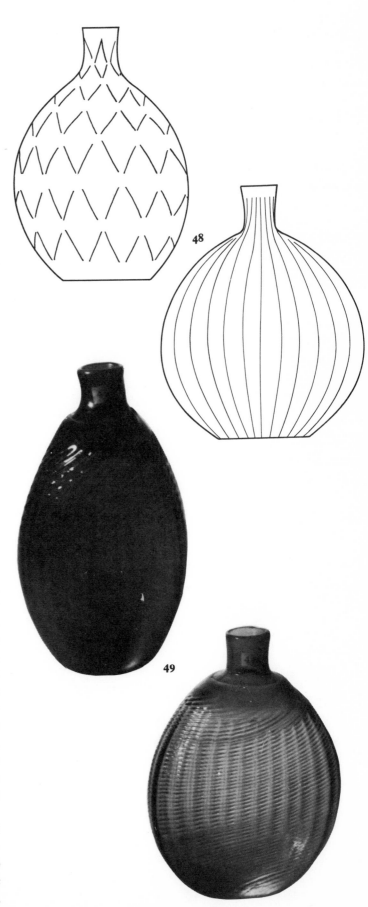

The Pitkin has a flattened, oval shape and narrow ribs, either vertical or swirled. The ribbing was achieved from a pattern mould and was usually doubled up from a second dip into the molten glass for additional strength. The combination of vertical and swirled ribbing is called broken swirl.

The name Pitkin became attached to this type of flask because early collectors assumed that they had only been made by the Pitkin Glass Works at Manchester, Connecticut, in the early years of the nineteenth century. It now seems that they were made throughout Connecticut and in at least one New Hampshire factory. There is, in fact, no proof other than the oral tradition that they were ever made at the Pitkin Works. The name has stuck, however, and been given to flasks of the same type found in the mid-west—Ohio, Pennsylvania and West Virginia. The eastern Pitkins from Connecticut and New Hampshire tend to have thirty-two or thirty-six ribs, and are primarily olive ambers and olive greens in colour. Those made in the mid-western factories have anything from sixteen to forty-four ribs, and are found in various shades of green, light to dark amber and aquamarine.

The chestnut-type of flask has a flattened, roundish body and is also pattern-moulded, but this time in a wider range of patterns: delicately formed diamond shapes, daisies in diamonds, or more rarely in hexagons, wide ribbing with a melon-like effect and the closer ribbing of the Pitkin-type, sometimes in the broken swirl design and occasionally with a distinct corn-on-the-cob effect. An attractive effect was often obtained by expanding the moulded pattern with a little more blowing. It is possible that some were made by William Henry Stiegel at Manheim in Pennsylvania in the late eighteenth century. A wide range of extraordinarily beautiful colours is associated with Ohio and other mid-western works during the early years of the nineteenth century—ambers, greens and occasionally blues. A globular shape, not flattened that is, and sometimes with a longer neck is also found in some of these patterns in a variety of sizes.

The pictorial and historical flasks were produced in vast quantities from about 1820 to 1870, although the pre-1850 ones are considered more desirable. The usual size is about a pint.

The flasks in the pictorial group—the smaller of the two—have such decorative motifs as dramatic sunbursts, cornucopias and double scrolls moulded on to them front and back. The latter also determines the shape of the flask. Common colours are aquamarine,

51

50 Mid nineteenth century mould-blown flasks carried designs to commemorate events and people. The violin-shaped flask on the left of the middle row is a 'Jenny Lind'.

light green and olive greens and ambers.

The historical group carries portraits of presidents, national heroes and various other characters; the emblems and symbols of national sovereignty, or those of political parties or other organisations and societies such as the Masons; and various inscriptions, famous sayings, or popular slogans.

The most common emblem by far is the American eagle, followed by George Washington and General Zachary Taylor, who performed well in the war against Mexico in the 1840s and proceeded to run successfully for president. Two lines associated with Taylor and the Mexican war also appear on a number of the flasks: 'General Taylor never surrenders' and 'A little more grape, Captain Bragg'—the encouragement said to have been given by Taylor to one of his officers at a crucial moment in the war.

One particularly significant flask records the deaths of Thomas Jefferson and John Adams—both by an extraordinary coincidence on the same day, and perhaps even more uncannily on the anniversary of the country's birth—4th July, 1826—exactly fifty years after Jefferson's Declaration of Independence had been signed. The inscription had been added to a mould showing Washington on one side and the eagle on the other.

Only two women ever appear on the historical flasks: a ballet dancer called Fanny Elssler who gained fame in the 1840s, and a visiting Swedish singer, Jenny Lind, who made a triumphant two-year tour of the country in the 1850s. But one of the most delightful symbolic heads is that of a woman, dubbed Columbia, the American Goddess of Liberty. She is seen in profile, wispy curls trailing down into her neck from under a soft cap.

One of the most prolific makers of the historical flasks was a man called Thomas William Dyott. His are among the most sought after by collectors because they are among the very few which can be identified with any certainty. But of his vast output from about 1818 to 1838, only a fraction has so far come to light with an identifying inscription, initials, or conclusive mould evidence.

It seems that Dyott arrived in Philadelphia as a young man, in about 1804, and first went into business as a druggist, later taking upon himself the title 'Doctor'—a common practice on both sides of the Atlantic. He seems to have soon become dissatisfied with the bottles locally available to him and gone into the business himself in about 1818. The first evidence we have that he was making historical flasks comes

from an advertisement in 1822. His own portrait appears on a number of the flasks. He had Benjamin Franklin keep him company on the other side!

One particular Dyott flask, which most collectors are on the look-out for, has the head of the French General Lafayette on one side and that of Washington on the other. It was mentioned specifically in one of the good doctor's advertisements in the early 1820s and has never come to light. Dyott, himself, apparently presented Lafayette with a commemorative one-pint pocket flask for brandy, with the General's head on one side and the U.S. coat-of-arms on the other, during Lafayette's triumphant visit to the Republic in 1824.

Bottle production seems to have been continued at the Dyottville works, founded by Thomas William, even after he went bankrupt in 1837. The existence of at least one flask with Dyott's initials filled-in suggest that someone else acquired his moulds.

After about 1850, portrait flasks became less common and less well designed—a deterioration in the mould-making which seems to have set in some years earlier.

The most characteristic shape of these flasks is a flattened oval—some more expansive than others—with a short neck and a plain lip. Some of the later flasks have a tapering rectangular look and others look quite like flattened case bottles, only wider, and with varying neck lengths. The gourd-shaped calabash with a long slender neck, and holding roughly one quart, seems to have made its appearance after about 1850.

One of the last series to be made celebrates the gold rush into Colorado in 1858. These bottles were made as late as 1870. They generally have a flattened rectangular shape and are embossed with the figure of a prospector carrying his tools over his shoulder and such inscriptions as 'For Pike's Peak', or 'Pike's Peak or Bust'.

As with the pictorial group, the most common colours are aquamarine and light green, sometimes olive amber and olive green; occasionally blues. Reproductions can often be detected by the brilliance of the colours—amethysts, blues, greens and ambers.

Three other types of whisky bottles are also attracting the collector's interest in the United States of America: those used by the Bininger Company of New York, the old log cabins of E. G. Booz—no less—a Philadelphia whisky vendor, and the Flora Temple Flasks, also made in Philadelphia.

The Bininger bottles are found in a great variety of

shapes—square, clock-shaped, barrel-shaped, flattened pear-shaped—and are extensively embossed. They come in most shades of amber and green with several known in puce—a very rare bottle colour. Some of the earliest bottles used by the company were imported from Bristol.

51 The E. G. Booz Old Cabin Whiskey bottles in the shape of log cabins were first produced about 1860. One method, though by no means fool-proof, of telling a reproduction, of which there have been many, is to check for the full stop after the word Whiskey. If it is not there, the chances are that it is a fake or a later copy. The really late copies, made after the end of Prohibition in 1933, carry the inscription 'Federal Law Forbids Sale or Re-use of this Bottle', an inscription which all liquor bottles had to carry by law until 1964. The earliest Booz cabins are amber. Later reproductions are again identified by brilliant and unusual colours such as blue, green, purple and yellow. At least one reproduction is known in milk-glass.

The Flora Temple flasks honour a great horse of that name, a trotter of mixed thoroughbred and saddle-horse stock, who won ninety-five of the one hundred and twelve races she entered and managed to break five records while she was about it. It was to commemorate the last of these records—a time of two minutes and nineteen and three-quarter seconds for the mile at Kalamazoo, Michigan, on 15th October 1859—that the Lancaster Glass Works, near Philadelphia, issued the flasks that bear the lady's portrait. The most common are dark green and have a small handle, but a pint-sized green is known without a handle.

Towards the end of the century, and until Prohibition began in 1920, small bottles ranging from half a pint down to one ounce, popularly called nips, were given away by merchants at holiday and special events. They were made in numerous animal, human and other shapes, as well as in other materials besides glass. It is not certain which contained spirits and which perfume. One rather portly little soldier, for example, is often classified with the perfumes, but seems a more appropriate subject for the stronger stuff.

Modern American whisky bottles that have a strong following are the ornamental types issued by the Jim Beam Co. of New Jersey. Interest in these was aroused when the company issued a glass cocktail shaker/decanter for the 1952/53 holiday celebrations. A series of so-called glass specialities has

52 Whisky bottle in ornamental glass issued by the Jim Beam Distillery Co., Chicago.

53 A pair of Bristol blue decanters made in about 1800 and decorated in gilt, with simulated labels inscribed: 'Rum' and 'Brandy'. A fine and rare pair. (Pilkington Glass Museum, St Helens, Lancashire).

52 been issued since then, but it appears not to be as popular as other series in pottery. Other companies, keeping up with the Beams, have also begun to market their whiskies and other alcoholic beverages in ornamental bottles. This has led to what might be called the Battle of the Bottles. One company, in opting for a plain old bottle, stated rather testily, but not without some justification, that the finest gift container was the one that contained the finest whisky. Who knows which will intrigue later generations of collectors?

In the first eleven years of this century, many a bottle containing spirits or other alcoholic beverages came under the hatchet of Mrs Carrie Nation, one of the architects of Prohibition, and one of America's most fanatical female demonstrators. Her campaign was waged not just across the United States of America but in Britain, Canada and Mexico, too. Mrs Nation appears to have had good reason to be worked up about the evils of alcohol. Her first husband, Dr Charles Gloyd, who had been a surgeon in the Civil War, was stoned, as the saying goes, when he led her to the altar and died shortly thereafter. Poor Carrie—her second husband divorced her on the grounds of desertion during the height of her campaign! The very American words, saloon and liquor, somehow still manage to express something of the degradation associated with excessive consumption of the waters of life.

Spirits were sold legally, and much more illegally, of course, during the Prohibition era in America, which lasted thirteen years as an amendment to the Constitution from 1920 to 1933, and much longer in some States. The labels on the legal bottles seem to have carried an odd combination of stricture or admonition, 'For medicinal purposes only', and titillation—the people in the illustrations are having a fine time and do not appear to need a doctor!

decanters

In the seventeenth century the greenish brown bottles, which were used to carry home wine, beer, spirits and liqueurs from the local merchant, were also used to serve the same beverages at the table. But something new and more elegant in the way of serving bottles was started in Britain when George Ravenscroft invented his clear glass, although he himself simply drew attention to his bottles as being 'extraordinary ware'. The name *decanter* for these special clear glass bottles seems to have come into general use in the early part of the eighteenth century. A raven's head seal was authorised for Ravenscroft's products by the London Glass Sellers' Company, which set him up in business.

The earliest decanter/bottles in Britain did not have stoppers. That refinement seems to have been **54** added in about 1735 to 1740, and remained an integral part of the design of these vessels thereafter. They are more valuable today if they still have their original stoppers. But making that judgment is not at all an easy task. Even experts have trouble.

Decanters are not the type of bottle likely to be found at the bottom of a rubbish dump, although they might have sunk into the ground along with many another treasured possession in an abandoned homestead. Rare things do turn up in odd places to confound us all, and make treasure-hunting the fun it is.

About the middle of the eighteenth century, decanters began to grow slimmer just as bottles did, but whereas wine bottles developed straight sides decanters kept more flowing, tapering lines. About 1775 a barrel-shaped body ousted all other forms from favour and subsequently became the characteristic shape made in the Irish factories at Cork, and Waterford as well. More rectangular and cylindrical shapes are found in the nineteenth century. It seems that these were kept locked away, but visible, in what was appropriately called a tantalus on many a Victorian sideboard.

Dark blue decanters, thought to have been made at Bristol around the turn of the eighteenth century, have delicately tapering sides and are decorated with gilt chains and labels indicating their contents. One **53** such label indicates a mysterious beverage called 'Shrub'. This was actually a liqueur or cordial, usually made of orange and lemon juice and rum.

Engraving was a common form of decoration

54 Bottle decanter in brownish soda glass, made in England in 1665. (Pilkington Glass Museum, St Helens, Lancashire).

55 The need to safeguard the contents of decanters and bar bottles led to several ingenious inventions for locking bottles.

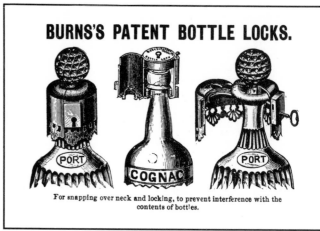

on the earliest British decanters and deep cutting on the later barrel shape. Enamelling was rare but was practised with particular delicacy by William and Mary Beilby of Newcastle upon Tyne, who always seem to have included a butterfly in their designs.

It is not yet possible to distinguish the special characteristics of the decanters made in New York, Baltimore, Philadelphia, Boston and Pittsburgh, but some fairly firm attributions have been made. Delicate copper-wheel engraving on slim, tapering decanters is characteristic of the work of Frederick Amelung at New Bremen, Maryland. A pineapple design is associated with New England pressed glass and a cut strawberry diamond and fan pattern with the Bakewell Company of Pittsburgh. Characteristic of the American output in the nineteenth century are the numerous geometric, Baroque, arch, fern and leaf designs of the three-part mould-blown ware of the period in which many decanters were made. Three-part moulds with similar patterns, however, were also widely used in France, so many a piece thought to be American might have been imported.

Towards the end of the nineteenth century in America, it became common practice for distillers to give away bar bottles to tavern owners who bought their liquor in bulk. One such type of bottle currently attracting the collector's interest has sunken panels displaying rather sentimental pictures of contemporary theatrical stars or colourful scenes sealed under a curved piece of glass. The names of bars, restaurants and hotels are also included in the decoration, at times. These bottles are mostly clear glass with cylindrical or slightly tapering bodies. In 1897 the Hayner Distilling Company in Ohio patented a rather unusual feature for their bar bottle—a combination lock stopper. This is one of the few bottles that can be locked! **55**

56 Medieval apothecaries made drugs from dried plants or herbs and stored the infusions in bulbous bottles with long necks.

57 Some chemists' shops still have show bottles on display and they were certainly present in Victorian chemists' shops.

medicine bottles

The medicine bottles that have survived from ancient Egypt and Mesopotamia, and are roughly dated about 1500 to 1350 BC, are among the oldest types of glass bottles known today. The Romans used glass for their medicines, too, and even in medieval Europe, when few other types of glass vessels seem to have been made, most of what was went to apothecaries and alchemists. A characteristic bottle of that period was the urinal with its almost timeless shape–a bulbous body with a long neck. Other small, crudely formed medicine bottles were known in fifteenth-century Tudor England, a common shape being a thin
56 cone with narrow shoulders and a short narrow neck. Tall case bottles were also used by apothecaries, which is probably one reason why gin was first bottled in them, as mentioned above.

The term *drug* comes from a Dutch word *droog*, meaning *dry*, and was probably extended to medicines because most early drugs were made from dried plants or herbs. Medieval apothecaries were treating heart disease with a preparation from the dried leaves of the purple foxglove long before the discovery of *digitalis*, a modern drug made from foxglove leaves.

The show bottles of coloured liquids which used to
57 stand in chemists' shops, and still do in many American shops, are the descendants of the large containers in which apothecaries steeped their herbs to extract the drugs–a process of maceration that sometimes went on for several days. The attractive power of the mysterious glass bottle standing in the window, combined with the magical powers of the product it contained, was obviously good for business.

By the middle of the eighteenth century more than two hundred patent and proprietary medicines were circulating in Britain, many of them packaged in quite characteristic glass bottles. These were medicines which had either a patent on the basis of their ingredients or a registered brand name.

One of the earliest such medicines known on both sides of the Atlantic was Turlington's Balsam of Life. In a 46-page booklet issued in about 1747, the inventor, Robert Turlington, asserted grandly that men of learning and genius had ransacked the animal, mineral and vegetable world in search of the remedy provided by 'the Author of Nature' for every malady. His own search, as one of that hallowed band, had led him to the Balsam, 'a perfect Friend of Nature, which

it strengthens and corroborates when weak and declining, vivifies and enlivens the Spirits, mixes with the Juices and Fluids of the Body and gently infuses its kindly Influence into those Parts that are most in Disorder.' Similar grandiose claims were to be made by each and every one of the hundreds and thousands of patent medicines which during the course of the next century and a half were offered to suffering humanity on both sides of the Atlantic.

The rather unusual bottle used for Turlington's cure-all scarcely changed during that time. It had a short, thick neck with stepped sides, first widening the body of the bottle and then narrowing it again at the base. Although Turlington had patented the Balsam in 1744, the characteristic shape of the bottle was not adopted until 1754, by which time it was necessary 'to prevent the Villainy of some Persons who buying up my empty Bottles, have basely and wickedly put therein a vile spurious Counterfeit-Sort [of Balsam]'. Such were the trials of competition even at that early date.

British soldiers might have had their Turlington's in their knapsacks during the Revolutionary War, but the embattled farmers may have been deprived of any such solace, although there is some evidence that some medicines were slipped through the British blockade of shipping in unmarked cases in the black of night. A trader in western Canada in 1783 when shot by a rival called for Turlington's Balsam to stop the bleeding, it is said, but, alas, to no avail.

A Turlington bottle was found in an Indian grave at Mobridge, South Dakota, and is now preserved at the Smithsonian Institution in Washington.

Only five other British patent medicines were widely known in the American colonies in the eighteenth century: Dalby's Carminative, Steer's Opodeldoc, Bateman's Pectoral Drops, Betton's British Oil, and Godfrey's Cordial. Dalby's Carminative was one of those that are 'allow'd to be the best thing that can be for ye Flux' and the many other misfortunes that the human body and mind are heirs to. Steer's Opodeldoc had a name supposedly coined by the Swiss physician Paracelsus, in the sixteenth century, for various medical plasters but appropriated by Dr Steer as a 'speedy and certain cure' for bruises, sprains, burns, cuts, chilblains, headaches and 'the Bite of venomous Insects' among other ills. The name was, not surprisingly, often mis-spelt, rather charmingly as 'Ofodeldo' in one early nineteenth-century advertisement. The bottles themselves kept a characteristic shape over many years.

58 A selection of medicine bottles found on old rubbish dumps in England in the Midlands. The tall bottle with sloping shoulders is quite a collector's piece. It contained Warner's Safe Cure, a patent medicine made in New York in the 1880s. This is embossed with 'London' and is one of the bottles which the company sold abroad. Warner's sold out in the early 1890s to the Duffy Company of Whisky Distillers. (Roy Morgan Collection).

59 The evolution of the medicine bottle. The bottle on the left, made in the seventeenth century, shows the 'kick up' caused by the pontil pushing the base up into the bottle.

60 A collection of miniature bottles, some with dropper lips. (Roy Morgan Collection).

59

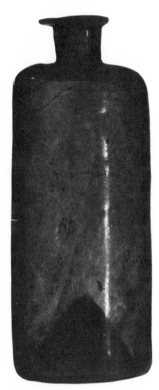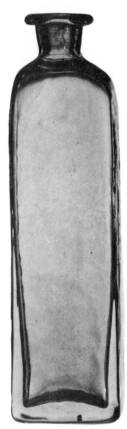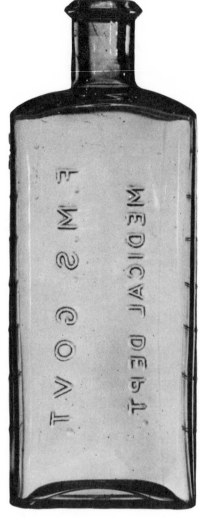

60

62

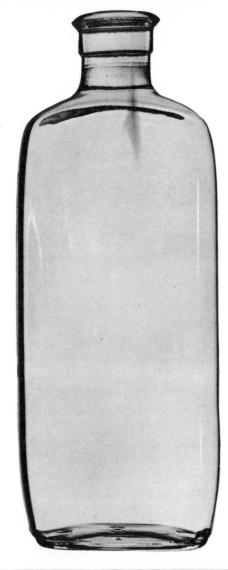

The actual contents of that handful seem to have been manufactured on these shores long before any attempt was made to copy the distinctive glass bottles by which they were easily recognised on the shelves of the sundry tradesmen who stocked them. And even after the thirteen colonies along the eastern seaboard had become an independent Republic, full and empty bottles of Turlington's Balsam of Life, among others, were still being imported.

In the early part of the nineteenth century our friend, Dr Thomas William Dyott of Philadelphia, had a very poor opinion of American-made bottles: 'so rude and shapeless . . . that purchasers seldom could be found if a foreign article could be obtained.' Some of the bottles the good doctor used for his own concoctions seem to have been made locally in his private mould as early as 1809. Two rectangular bottles have been recorded with the inscription, 'Dr Robertson's Family Medicine Prepared only by T. W. Dyott.' Not long after that he was manufacturing his own bottles 'in quality and workmanship . . . equal and in many of the articles superior to the English manufacture.'

From about 1818 to 1838, Dyott produced vast quantities of medicine bottles at his own glass-works. In an 1825 advertisement he listed certain types of bottles by the thousands of gross, and it was not long before he had agents throughout the country. He made bottles for the old British stand-bys mentioned above and for the newer local nostrums that began edging the imports out of the way, and, of course, the larger demijohns and carboys used for transporting each and all, hither and thither.

By about the middle of the nineteenth century, all sorts of fanciful local products were flooding the market, in cylindrical, oval, rectangular and panelled bottles and the copywriters on both sides of the Atlantic were rivalling their English counterparts from the eighteenth century in eloquent claims for their product and vitriol for all rivals and counterfeiters. Towards the end of the century, the enterprising Kickapoo medicines were touring Europe and Australia with their wares. And the medicine show became a popular event. It is not surprising that some of the showmen switched over into the theatre proper. John A. Hamlin, for example, whose brain child had been Wizard Oil, renowned as a treatment for muscular ailments, once owned the Grand Opera House in Chicago.

The proprietor's signature on the label, and later his portrait, were widely believed to be their personal guarantee of the product. If a man was willing to put his name and face on a package he could not be ashamed of the contents – so the sick and the malingering wanted to believe.

Any medicine bottle with the name 'Shaker' embossed on it is much sought after by today's collectors. The Shakers were an ascetically religious sect who set up self-contained communities mainly in the New England states during the nineteenth century. They sold many of their products to the outside world.

That good temperance people quietly tippled away at their favourite medicines or were persuaded of the medicinal virtues of such as Duffy's Pure Malt Whiskey is not really so surprising. Duffy's had been declared a patent medicine by the U.S. government when it was raising the money for the Spanish-American War in the Caribbean in the 1890s through a special tax on nostrums. The company could later claim with some justification that its product was 'the only whisky recognised by the Government as a medicine.' In the seventeenth century the English physician, Thomas Sydenham, had said without opium medicine would be a one-armed man. But by the end of the nineteenth century, there was growing fear of such a powerful narcotic, particularly in the soothing syrups given to children.

The precise action of alcohol or opium or any of the numerous other ingredients of the patent medicines in combating disease was only hazily understood. With the establishment of the germ theory of disease, and other scientific discoveries in the nineteenth century, however, the therapeutic efficiency of the patent medicines could be more effectively measured and action taken to curb the extravagant claims made for them during the previous two centuries.

Given some of the frightful and unexpected side-effects of modern drugs, we can ill afford to scoff at the gullibility of our ancestors. With the advent of scientific medicine, moreover, something of the fantasy of the curative nostrums and their soothing and intriguing names – Balsams of Honey, Elixirs of Life, Dr Lin's Celestial Balm of China, Swaim's Panacea – has gone out of our lives. Apparently Lydia Pinkham's Vegetable Compound – devised by one of the rare women in the field for the ills of her sex – can still be obtained today. That one, however, no longer sounds very tempting. Fantasy in names seems to have moved over into perfume bottles, by way of compensation. I recently noticed an advertisement for the 'mysterious black bottles of Zen' – a Japanese import.

62 Even when bitters bottles still looked like bottles they took on a great variety of shapes.

63 One of the many exotic shapes used for bitters bottles. An amber glass bottle in the shape of a pig. 1860 to 1870. (Philadelphia Art Museum, Pennsylvania. Bequest of R. Wistar Harvey).

64 A collection of mineral water bottles showing a variety of shapes and attempts at closure—internal screw stopper, marble stopper and a Hamilton bottle designed to lie on its side to keep the cork moist. (Mary Lindsay Collection).

bitters bottles

A special category of medicine bottles called 'bitters' has become particularly popular with collectors. In fact, so many are now turning up—over thirty-five brands have so far been identified for the California area alone in the last thirty-odd years of the nineteenth century—that interest is apparently beginning to wane.

Bitters were no less extravagant than elixirs and balsams and other proprietary medicines in their claims to cure all ills. They were also mostly more than 50 per cent alcohol. However, in the post Civil War years, as more and more people struggled with the dictates of the temperance movement and their need for liquid courage or tranquillisers, bitters became more socially acceptable.

The idea of impregnating liquors with a bitter substance such as angostura, quassia, or bitter orange rind, and flavouring them with juniper, cinnamon, caraway, camomile, cloves, and so on, as a means of promoting digestion or appetite or as a tonic, was an old one in medicine. In eighteenth-century England, gin salesmen got around the Government's tax on their liquor by adding various herbs and calling it Bitters, Coltick Water and Gripe Water. One such enterprising fellow, when dragged into court to account for himself and the popularity of his product, explained that the new tax on gin had given so many people the cholic that they needed his medicine!

During the Civil War in the United States of America, one Dr J. Hostetter persuaded the Government to substitute his Celebrated Stomach Bitters for whisky and quinine as an invigorant. It was more than 47 per cent alcohol at the time, apparently.

Many other ingredients were used, but the alcoholic rather than the herbal content got the headline in such as Pure Apple Brandy Bitters, Bourbon Whiskey Bitters and Clarke's Vegetable Sherry Wine Tonic Bitters.

Some bitters were bottled in rather plain, upright, rectangular containers, but many were put into bottles that took all sorts of shapes and forms: **62** barrels, log cabins, ears of corn, fish, lighthouses, **63** balls, drums, frankfurters, cigars, soldiers. An Indian Princess, much prized by collectors, held Brown's Celebrated Indian Herb Bitters. The New York **61** Artillery Bitters, appropriately enough, went into a cannon bottle, a rather rare shape.

The most common colours for bitters bottles are shades of amber, aquamarine, clear, and a wide range of greens. The rare ones are blue, puce, amethyst and milk-glass.

mineral & soda-water bottles

Thousands of mineral water springs, some of which
are naturally carbonated, are scattered around the
world and have been used since ancient times to treat
such ailments as rheumatism, skin infections and poor
digestion. By about the end of the seventeenth
century it was becoming popular for the nobility in
Europe to visit the health resorts that were growing up
around these springs 'to take the waters', or 'for the
cure' of any and all ailments, slight or serious. This
often meant bathing in, as well as drinking of, the
wonderful waters.

Tsar Peter the Great's visit to Spa, in what is now
Belgium, around the turn of the seventeenth century,
brought such fame to the waters there that a bottle
was made especially for them by glass factories in and
around Liège, and the name, spa, began to be applied
to any place where there was a mineral spring.

By the end of the eighteenth century, fashionable
watering places – a name applied to spas and seaside
resorts – had blossomed around springs throughout
65 Europe: Baden-Baden in Germany, Karlsbad (now
Karlovy Vary) and Marienbad in what is now Czecho-
68 slovakia, Aix-les-Bains in France, Bath and Harrogate in England; and by the early part of the nine- **69**
teenth century around various springs in the United
States of America, too. Saratoga, in northern New
York state, is one of the more famous, but there were
others: Blount Springs, the Saratoga of the South,
near Huntsville, Alabama, and Jackson's Napa Soda
Springs and Bartlett Springs in California.

Artificially carbonated water was first produced in
a practical manner in the late eighteenth century by
the English chemist, Joseph Priestley, when he
invented a method for dissolving carbon dioxide in
water. Priestly emphasised the medicinal virtues in
artificially carbonated water, but they were later
found to be illusory.

Manufacturers of artificial mineral waters – carbonated and non-carbonated – were in business shortly
after Priestley's discovery. Priestley himself was perse-
cuted for his political views and sought refuge in the
United States of America where he died in 1804.
In 1794, Jacob Schweppe, a Swiss, set up one such
business in Bristol. He first used earthenware bottles,
but soon switched to glass. The first recorded patent
for an imitation mineral water in the United States
was granted to Joseph Hawkins of the firm of Shaw
and Hawkins in Philadelphia in 1809.

The bottling of artificially carbonated water on a
large scale in America is associated with the name of

66 Soda-water bottles from Honolulu with Hutchinson spring wire stoppers. (Rex Elliott Collection).

67 Some modifications of the Codd-stopper bottle. A collection found in England in the Midlands. (Roy Morgan Collection).

68 An unusual, dump-like, bung stopper bottle for Harrogate Spa water. Almost certainly nineteenth century. (Roy Morgan Collection).

69 An example of the dump-shaped bung stopper, seltzer bottle – the first glass bottle to be used for mineral waters in England. (Roy Morgan Collection).

70 Colour variations in Codd-stopper
bottles: amber, brown, dark green, light
blue, clear glass and standard aqua green
(bottle in foreground with crown
trademark). (Roy Morgan Collection).

A PROPHYLACTIC AGAINST CHOLERA.

"LEMONADE IN A MOMENT"
WITH PLAIN OR AERATED WATERS.

CARTER'S
EXTRA CONCENTRATED

LEMON
THE ORIGINAL
Established
·1831·
DRY OR

SYRUP.
Superior to
LIME JUICE
CORDIAL
SWEET.

EXTRA
LEMON
CONCENTRATED

FOUNDED 1831
Carter's Bristol
FRUIT SYRUPS

H.W. CARTER & CO LTD The Old Refinery, BRISTOL·

GOES FARTHEST - THEREFORE CHEAPEST.
SAMPLE BOTTLES. LARGE,1 3; 1 DOZ CASE 13/- CARRIAGE PAID ON RECEIPT OF CASH.

72 The characteristic hobble-skirt shape of today's Coca-Cola bottle has remained practically unchanged since it was introduced in 1915. Prior to that a variety of shapes, colours and embossments are found as seen here.

John Matthews, an immigrant Englishman who set up shop in New York about 1830. He introduced the use of marble chips in making carbonated water and to that end acquired all the scrap marble left over from the building of St Patrick's Cathedral in New York!

Almost inevitably there was some confusion in the terminology used for the natural mineral waters and the substitutes devised for them. The name seltzer, for example, was first applied to the medicinal mineral water found at Selters in Germany, and then more generally to the artificial substitutes for it. Our friend, Dr Dyott of Philadelphia, was advertising Seltzer bottles as early as 1816. The name soda-water seems to have grown out of the early use of sodium bicarbonate to make an effervescent drink and then became limited – in America at least – to the substitutes, particularly after they began to be coloured and flavoured. In 1843 such incomprehensible and mouth-watering flavours as 'Sarsaparilla, lemon, ginger, pine apllea [sic], winter green, orgeat, strawberry, raspberry, blackberry, peach and vanilla' were being advertised. **71** Orgeat was simply a mixture of barley or almond extract with orange-flower water. Sarsaparilla was a tropical shrub found especially in Jamaica. The flavour seems to have been extracted from the dried roots.

There seem to be no distinctions between the bottles used for the natural mineral waters and those used for the substitutes. Some are like the small wine or beer of the late eighteenth century with a cylindrical body, straight sides, squared-off shoulders, and short cylindrical neck. Others have slimmer proportions with tapering shoulders, again similar to bottles used for beer. Common colours for mineral and soda-water bottles are olive green, olive amber, some light greens, aquamarine and clear. A mysterious advertise- **70** ment of the early 1800s listed a red mineral bottle as well as blue and green. No red has so far come to light in America, and little else is known about the company who advertised it: the Eagle Glass Works of Claridge and Rudolph in Philadelphia.

A cobalt blue – the dark colour was believed to have preservative powers – peddled on trains and shipped to many towns in Alabama and Tennessee in the 1870s, was a popular bottle for the waters of Blount Springs, Alabama.

One New York mineral water bottle is found in green, amber, black and olive yellow. Such an unusual variety of colours has led to speculation that a different colour may have been used for each of the springs from which water was gathered, but there is as yet

73 A collection of mineral water bottles. The second from the left is a Thwaites full Codd-stopper bottle—the marble is held in position against the rubber ring. Others show various types of closure common in the Irish trade. (Guinness Museum, Dublin).

little evidence to substantiate the theory. The springs are known collectively as the Oak Orchard Acid Springs and are situated in the town of Alabama, New York. When the first white man came upon the springs in 1816, neither he nor his horse seems to have cared much for them, but by the 1840s a flourishing health resort was attracting the crowds.

As with beer, there was the problem of corks popping. To combat that problem an Englishman, William Hamilton, patented an egg-shaped bottle which had to be stored on its side. That meant that the cork would always be kept moist and consequently would not pop. The Hamilton bottle was patented in 1814 but did not become popular until the 1840s, after which time it was considered essential for soda-water until the end of the century. A modified form of the egg-shape, known as the flat-egg because of its flat bottom, was patented in 1870. It could be stored either upright or on its side. The name egg is not entirely appropriate—it is a very elongated-looking egg, and collectors sometimes refer to these bottles as torpedoes. They are not unlike tenpins, skittles or Indian clubs, depending on one's point of view. A glass-maker in New Jersey, in 1845, complained that egg minerals were very difficult to make. In Britain they are often called Hamiltons.

One of the most unusual shapes for mineral water bottles was devised by Hiram Codd of London in 1872 and patented in the United States of America in 1873. Its peculiar shape was the result of the type of stopper Codd had devised and is centred around the short shoulders of the bottle, where the glass is pinched inwards to hold the glass marble which constituted the stopper. The marble was kept pressed against a rubber ring by the gas pressure of the beverage. The term 'Codd's wallop' was used contemptuously by British beer drinkers for the waters bottled in Codd's invention, which became the most widely used type of bottle for carbonated soft drinks in Britain in the twenty-odd years preceding the beginning of World War I. Children went after the marbles, of course, so other types of internal stoppers were subsequently patented. This type of bottle is apparently still being manufactured in the Far East today.

64

67

74 'General Taylor Never Surrenders' –
a flask commemorating General Zachary
Taylor in the Mexican War. (Private
Collection).

74 'General Taylor Never Surrenders' –
a flask commemorating General Zachary
Taylor in the Mexican War. (Private
Collection).

75 The soda-water syphon was invented in 1813 by Charles Plynth, who called it the 'portable fountain'. When the top was released the pressure of gas in the bottle forced the liquid out through the tube. (Roy Morgan Collection).

76 A Moses bottle. One of the more unusual bottles made in America for mineral waters from Poland Spring, Maine. It was first issued in 1876. (Brooklyn Museum, New York. Gift of Mrs Alberta P. Locke).

77 The Swedish glassmaking firm of
Orrefors showed this cut glass carafe and
flask at the Paris Exhibition of 1925.
(Musée des Arts Décoratifs, Paris).

One of the more unusual bottles made in America for mineral waters is called a Moses bottle and is shaped in the figure of that ancient patriarch. It was used for the mineral water from Poland Spring in the state of Maine and is said to have been inspired by the story of Moses drawing water from a rock in Horeb. It is thought to have been first issued in about 1876 and does not seem to have had a long life. There are some thirty known varieties of the Moses bottle, among which are many copies of the original, at least three of which were issued prior to World War I. In the 1930s another was issued which contained gin.

The mineral water people were as extravagant in their claims for their products as their medicine friends.

Legend has it that many a wounded soldier felt the curative and sanitary virtues of the mineral water springs near the site of the Civil War battle of Gettysburg in Pennsylvania in 1863. Gettysburg Katalysine Spring Water was subsequently bottled and used to treat rheumatism, diabetes, kidney and urinary diseases, gout, dyspepsia and nervous diseases – to mention only a few.

In the late 1800s a number of resorts around mineral springs took to boasting about the lithium in their waters – no matter how infinitesimal the amounts – and emphasised its healing virtues. When the United States Government began investigating the claims of all medicines and medicinal waters early in this century, it was found that the amount of lithium in Buffalo Lithia Water, for example, could not even be weighed, and that it would have been necessary to drink two hundred thousand gallons of the stuff in order to obtain a therapeutic dose of lithium. Ah, truth in advertising! The 'lithia' was, needless to say, dropped from the title after that.

Coca-Cola actually started out in the 1880s as a cure for headache. The characteristic hobble-skirt shape of today's bottle had remained practically unchanged since it was introduced in 1915. Prior to that a variety of shapes, colours and embossments are found.   72

perfume & snuff bottles

The names for bottles in the perfume category vary enormously, as do their shapes and sizes, to say nothing of their decoration. They can be divided fairly easily, however, into the portable and non-portable: the small sizes which easily slipped into a pocket, glove or purse, or were carried around the wrist, and the larger sizes that stayed at home on the dressing-table or wash-stand or were kept at the   78 79 80

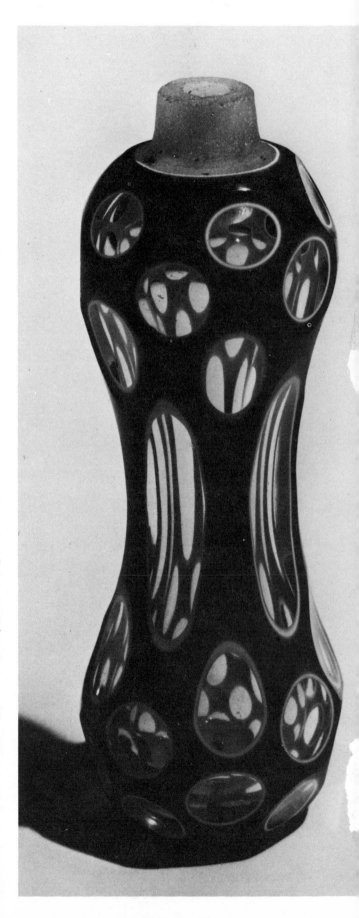

barber's shop. Snuff bottles also fall into two categories: the very decorative glass bottles made in China and the more ordinary, household bottles, which will be discussed later.

In addition to their hygienic and medicinal qualities—evident in such names as smelling and scent bottles and pungents—perfume bottles and their contents have played no small part in the art of seduction. In the eighteenth century, considered the great age of perfume bottles, they were the most important type of *Galanteriewaren*—a wonderfully self-explanatory word—that a gentleman could take to his lady love. But although some were made of glass, notably in Austria and France, the majority were wrought of more exotic materials, including fish skin, and consequently do not play a major part in this story.

Mrs Martha Washington, wife of the first President of the United States of America, is thought to have slipped into her glove a simple perfume bottle made by Caspar Wistar, the man who had set up America's first really successful glass-house in New Jersey, in 1739. But the earliest we know today are those attributed with some certainty to Henry William Stiegel, who set up his factories at Manheim in Pennsylvania in the 1760s.

Among the small sizes—$2\frac{1}{2}$ ins. to 3 ins. tall—are those that look like some kinds of sea-shells—narrow oval bodies with overall ribbing—and those that look like that strange little creature, the seahorse, only they do not have a head. But they do have a scaly back created either by a pinched trailing of applied glass, sometimes called quilling, or by thin, parallel ribs of glass, called rigaree. They also have a curled-around tail on which they sit. Both types are found in a wide variety of colours. On the latter the colour of the trailing decoration frequently contrasts with that of the body. Both were made by other glass-makers in the eighteenth and nineteenth centuries.

The big favourites among the perfume bottles attributed to Stiegel, however, are the fat little globular shapes with short necks, the type one could only hope to inherit, with any luck. One of the principal authorities on American glass, Helen McKearin, considers that these little bottles together with the mid-western chestnuts and globular shapes, mentioned under whisky bottles, have seldom been excelled or equalled for colour and delicacy of design. The designs were pattern-moulded and sometimes expanded with more blowing. A diamond and daisy pattern, the rare daisy-in-hexagon and the broken swirl have been noted only in America. The evidence points to Stiegel

having exclusive claim to the first two, just as he almost has on the amethyst colour. Other colours are rare.

Towards the end of the eighteenth century, opaque white, deep blue and green perfume bottles were being made at Bristol and elsewhere in Great Britain. They have a flattened rectangular shape and are decorated with pastoral scenes and floral motifs of Chinese inspiration in gilt and enamels. The white stripes and splashes on dark green glass, for example, associated with what is called Nailsea work from its assumed production in that town near Bristol, are found on very flat oval perfume bottles which taper almost to a point at the base. Some may have been made in America. The rare cameo glass perfume bottle occasionally found in America is assumed to be of English make, although cameo glass was made in America towards the end of the nineteenth century. One London glass-maker, Apsley Pellatt, was renowned for his cameo incrustations on perfume bottles, among others, early in the nineteenth century.

An attractive group of American toilet water bottles was blown in three-part moulds, principally in spiral and vertical ribbing patterns, in a variety of colours. Some of the colours are extremely rare: a dark red with amber streaks, a translucent lavender, blue in direct light, and a turquoise blue with opalescent tortoise-shell streaks.

It is rare for any piece shaped by Louis Comfort Tiffany to be called a bottle, but among those rare pieces are perfume bottles.

Among the plainer toilet water bottles are all those that once held hair balsams, dyes, renewers, invigorators, restorers, nourishers, lotions, washes, preservatives, unguents, oils and pomades, from which fortunes were made in the nineteenth century and are still being made. Among these are what are called barber bottles, in which hair tonics, like bay rum and witch-hazel, were kept. The more exotic of these, in a wide variety of colours, have been collected since the 1920s.

As cheaply moulded glassware became available towards the end of the nineteenth century, shapes grew more and more fanciful. Those in coloured glass are now most sought after.

After the introduction of tobacco into Europe, around the turn of the fifteenth century, and subsequently into China, snuff or tobacco in its powdered form—snuffing-tobacco as it is called in Dutch—was packaged in many different kinds of container. Boxes became the most popular in Europe, but bottles were

China's favourite, and some were made of glass. As with perfumes, the small sizes were for carrying around, and the larger ones for staying at home. Various decorative techniques were employed: plain or carved monochrome, inside or outside painting, cameo, overlay and mottles. It is not unusual, for example, to find as many as seven layers of glass, each one a different colour, and sometimes with paintings between the layers. Many so successfully imitate jade and other precious materials, that it is hard to distinguish them from the real mineral. Some of the finest in plain, opaque white or with delicately enamelled decoration bear the mark of Ku Yueh Hsuan, the man whose glass was imitated in porcelain. Most date from the eighteenth and nineteenth centuries.

general household bottles

Before the latter part of the nineteenth century very few foods could be preserved for winter eating or times of scarcity, other than dry substances such as chocolate powder and mustard—'genuine Flour of Mustard-seed of all Degrees of Fineness'—or pickles and sauces and other products that did not require a fully air-tight seal. Jams and jellies, for example, had sufficient sugar content to remain unspoilt without hermetic sealing.

It is thought that bottles similar to the eighteenth-century case bottles mentioned earlier as gin bottles, were made with a wide mouth and used for pickles. A similar type was also used for transporting snuff in large quantities, and powdered jalap, too. The majority of those known are made of plain, dark glass, unadorned except for an occasional elaborate paper label. Some large cylindrical bottles were probably also used for similar purposes. Early free-blown examples are rare; later mould-blown ones are more common.

A particular type of rectangular bottle, with a short neck, sometimes slightly rounded shoulders, sometimes more squared off, and occasionally with chamfered sides, was used for mustard, chocolate powder and snuff, as early as the eighteenth century and continued in use into the nineteenth century.

Some home preserving was done in the eighteenth century by boiling certain foods in 'pint glass jars . . .

81 Bottle for red cabbage, nineteenth century. (Blackburn Museum, Lancashire).

82 Wide-mouthed jars used for snuff.

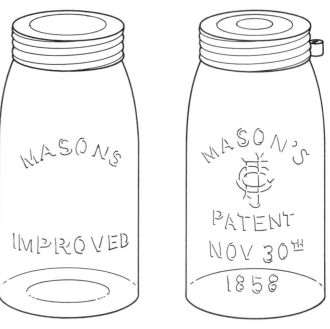

83 The first Mason jar was blown to the inventor's specifications in a small glass shop in New Jersey, but the famous line: 'Masons Patent. November 30 1858' was to be inscribed on preserving jars for the next three-quarters of a century.

with glass lids' later sealed down with carpenters' glue. But credit for expounding the principle of food preservation through heat and the elimination of air goes to Nicholas Appert, a Frenchman. The pre-cooked fruits, meats, fish and vegetables Appert had preserved in sealed glass jars were successfully put to the test during the Napoleonic Wars and Appert was awarded a substantial prize for his achievement. But the problem of a satisfactory closure remained until an American, John Landis Mason, invented his air-tight screw-topped jar in 1858. Widespread home preserving followed as a result of Mason's invention. This actually preceded Louis Pasteur's discovery that micro-organisms were responsible for food decay, that these could be destroyed by heat and that food consequently kept fresh in air-tight glass. Glass had been chosen by Appert as 'the material most impenetrable by air'.

The first Mason jar was blown to the inventor's specifications in a small glass shop in southern New Jersey, but the famous line, 'Mason's Patent, November 30, 1858', was to be inscribed on preserving jars 83 for the next three-quarters of a century. A large New York department store, capitalising on bottle interest and a recent nostalgic film of the World War II era, recently advertised such jars under the coy title, "Summer of '42 [the title of the film] or maybe '43 or '44." It is still possible to buy Mason jars, now a generic term, in Woolworth's and other dime stores, although not much in these stores costs ten cents any more.

The *Kilner* and similar jars did not come into general use in Britain until about the time of World War I.

Horse-radish was one of the first of the 'good things for the table' bottled by Henry J. Heinz when his company began modestly in 1869. Clear glass bottles were used to show that no turnip fill had been included. Heinz and his bottled products did much to build consumer confidence in foods not preserved at home.

The Gothic pickle bottle–a very popular one with collectors–made its appearance around the middle of the nineteenth century. It has four or sometimes six sunken panels with pointed arches, trefoils or elaborate tracery moulded into its sides, and sometimes smaller 86 ones moulded into the shoulders as well. It is found up to 17 ins. tall, mostly in rich aquamarines and ambers. One such bottle was recently unearthed with its contents intact–pickles, cucumbers, cauliflower, peppers, cherries–when the San Francisco water-front was being excavated for a new transit system.

84 Bottles for sauce, gravy browning, coffee extract, meat and fruit juices – all embossed with the name of their contents. (Roy Morgan Collection).

85 Cathedral-type pickle jars, with panels of a Gothic arch design, were produced in America for about forty years, between 1880 and 1920.

86 Cut glass cruet bottle, eighteenth century. (Victoria and Albert Museum, London).

83

85

84

86

Some peppersauce bottles also have the neo-Gothic details.

Caster bottles (that is, salts, shakers for sugar, cinnamon or pepper) and mustard pots and cruets for oil and vinegar are also found in a number of the three-part mould-blown and pressed-glass patterns. The honeycomb pattern of pressed glass, for example, is found on ketchup and peppersauce bottles, as well as syrup jugs. Such bottles are usually in clear glass, although pressed ware towards the end of the nineteenth century was also made in various colours.

Milk used to be delivered directly from cow or goat at the doorstep, then from the farmer's churn, and only towards the end of the nineteenth century in **89** glass bottles. They were not in widespread use on either side of the Atlantic, however, until after World War I. They have now virtually disappeared from the American scene–replaced by waxed paper cartons– and are in the process of disappearing in Britain. The milk bottle's life has been a short one.

The earliest known American bottle is the Thatcher Milk Protector–brain-child of Dr Harvey D. Thatcher, a druggist of Potsdam, New York. A Quaker **88** farmer, sitting milking a cow, is embossed on the body. The originals are extremely rare, but reproductions have been made in several colours and in clear glass.

The lightning-type of closure, sometimes aptly described as a swing stopper, was used on early milk **90** bottles. It was largely replaced towards the end of the century by paper caps fitted into a specially formed groove in the mouth of the bottle.

Dairies, large and small, could afford to have their **87** names embossed on their bottles.

The usual colour is clear, but amber was occasionally used on the old theory of using dark glass to prevent spoilage. White milk-glass is known, but only one green bottle.

89 The evolution of the milk bottle from the end of the nineteenth century to the present day.

90 Sterilised milk was bottled in swing stoppered bottles from 1894. Milk bottles became a vehicle for advertising – slogans could be applied to the bottle by a silk-screen process. (Unigate Museum, London).

A long neck is unusual on a milk bottle, except perhaps in France; so are eight sides, a wide mouth or a square shape.

Small candy bottles, ranging in height from one to several inches, and taking many shapes and forms, appeared in the latter part of the nineteenth century and are beginning to attract the collector's attention. One of the earliest known is shaped like the Liberty Bell preserved in Philadelphia's Independence Hall. Most are in clear glass, to show off the coloured candy inside. According to your fancy, you will find railroad lanterns, horns, suitcases, clocks, telephones, cars, planes, guns, locomotives, battleships and tanks, and the inevitable politicians' hats. A variety of closures were used.

One estimate made of the number of ink bottles currently attracting attention is that there are over one thousand types. Many of those are in unusual shapes: umbrellas, tea-kettles, shoes, turtles, barrels, buildings, people, boats. Common colours are aquamarine and light greens. Uncommon are various shades of amber, cobalt blue, amethyst and dark green. A rather rare and intriguing group are those patented for some kind of technical innovation. The master bottles or bulk containers always seem to have been made of poor quality glass with lots of bubbles and tears. Similar bottles seem to have been used for glue and shoe blacking.

Among the grimmer shapes and more luridly coloured bottles are those that once contained poison. One startling shape has a neck bent at a 90-degree angle. Dark blues and browns were considered readily identifiable colours. Other less startling shapes are ribbed, quilted and checkered in some way distinctive to the touch for ready identification in the dark. Somewhere around the 1930s it was decided that the unusual shapes and colours actually attracted the attention of children and more thought was given to safety closures.

miscellaneous & unusual bottles

Since bottles have been made in practically every shape and size you can think of, a good many of them are unusual. Many collectors like to concentrate on bottles shaped like something else—animal, vegetable or mineral. They might have contained practically

92 Spanish bottle of the seventeenth
century in greenish grey glass with
elaborate trailed and pincered decoration.
(Victoria and Albert Museum, London).

93 A gemel or twin flask in Nailsea glass
made in the late eighteenth century.
(Victoria and Albert Museum, London).

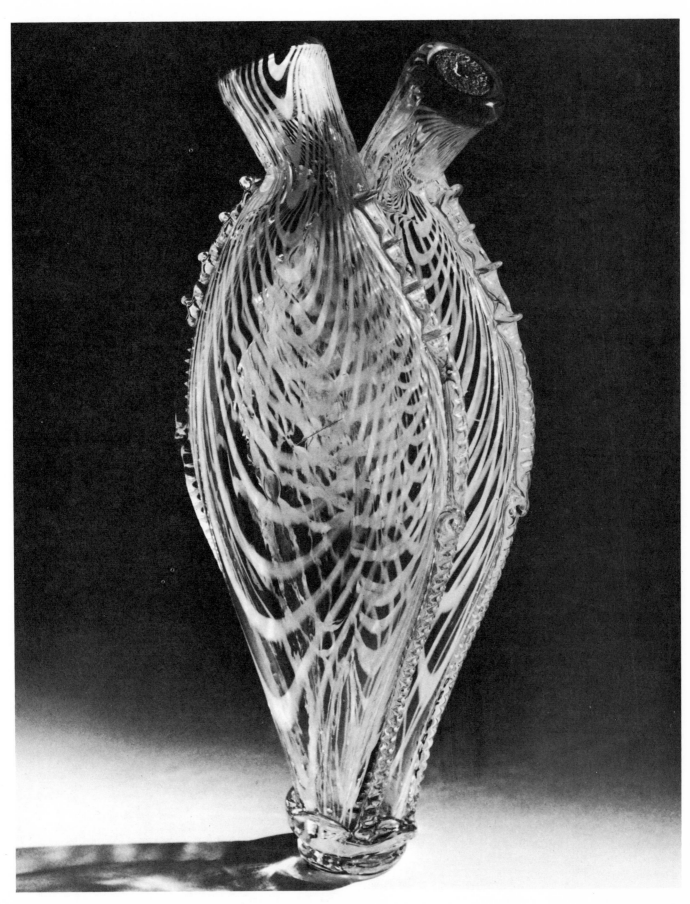

94 Inkwell made at Stourbridge at the time of the Great Exhibition of 1851. Base and stopper are decorated with concentric rings of red, white and blue millefiori canes.

95 The Lily-pad decoration is especially American—no European prototype is known. A hot gather of glass applied to the base of the vessel is pulled up around the sides.

96 This wine bottle was hand-painted in the 1920s by René Magritte. It was sold at Sotheby's in November, 1972 for £7,550 ($18,000).

97 Contemporary bottles designed to appeal to the collector.

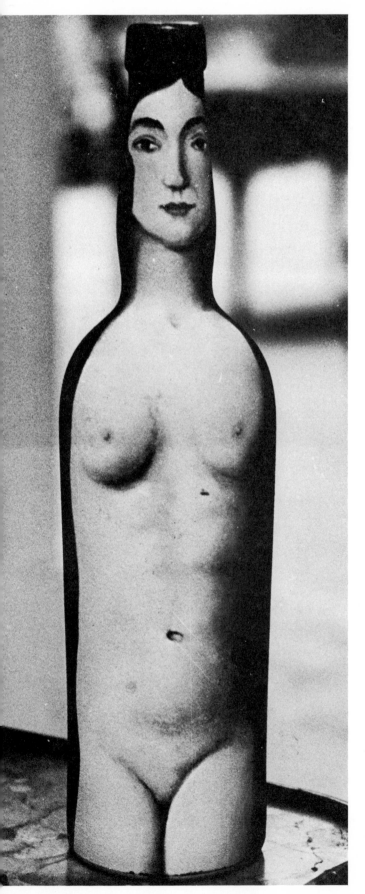

any of the liquids or solids mentioned above. No two collectors would probably ever agree on what are the most unusual.

My eye lingers over an intricately decorated unguentarium from the ancient Middle East. I am intrigued by the German *Kuttrolf* with its twisted neck controlling the flow of precious fluids to a drip; the Spanish *almorratxa* or rosewater sprinkler, bristling with pincered crestings and dripping with glass loops; a French Pilgrim bottle with a body shaped like a dough-nut; the double or gemel bottles **93** and those in the form of a bellows. I am charmed by the *porte perruque* or wig holder stopper of an eighteenth-century French toilet bottle and cherish an American powder-horn flask because it is a rare form and one of the few bottles to be decorated with the applied lily-pad design thought to be peculiar to **95** American-made glass. I feel festive at the sight of the British toddy-lifter. It has a very long thin neck and a hole in the bottom of its more portly body designed for lifting punch from a bowl. The beverage was released into a glass by removing the thumb from the mouth.

A group of bottles with an unusual function, rather than shape, are the target bottles used by marksmen in the nineteenth century. Their shape, in fact, is that of a simple ball. Colourful evidence of a hit was sometimes provided by filling them with feathers, ribbons, confetti or smoke. They were invented in England in the 1830s and used in the United States of America from about 1850 to 1880, when clay pigeons were invented. Not many have survived—for obvious reasons.

Happy hunting!

Bibliography

Acknowledgements

Cecil Munsey. *The Illustrated Guide to Collecting Bottles*. Hawthorn Books, New York, 1970.

Sheelah Ruggles-Brise. *Sealed Bottles*. Country Life, London, 1949.

Derek C. Davis. *English Bottles and Decanters, 1650–1900*. Letts, London, 1972.

John P. Adams. *Bottle Collecting in America*. N.H. Publishing Co., New Hampshire, 1971.

John P. Adams. *Third Guide to Identifying & Pricing Bottles*. N.H. Publishing Co., New Hampshire, 1972.

John P. Adams. *Bottle Collecting in New England*. N.H. Publishing Co., New Hampshire, 1971.

Edward Fletcher. *Bottle Collecting*. Blandford, London, 1972.

Bob Ashton. *Bottle Book*. Exposition Press, New York, 1972.

Ferol Austen. *Poor Man's Guide to Bottle Collecting*. Doubleday, New York, 1971.

Ferol Austen. *Bischoff Bottles*. Cembura & Avery, California, 1969.

Ferol Austen. *Garnier Bottles. Identification and Price Guide*. Cembura & Avery, California, 1969.

Ferol Austen. *Jim Beam Bottles*. Cembura & Avery, California, 1969.

Ferol Austen. *Luxardo Bottles*. Cembura & Avery, California, 1969.

Lynn Blumenstein. *Bottle Rush U.S.A.* Old Time Bottle Publishing Co., Salem, 1966.

John Edwards & Charles Gardner. *Collector's Price Guide to Historical Bottles and Flasks*. (Privately printed).

Bob & Pat Ferraro. *Bottle Collector's Book*. Past in Glass, Boulder City, 1966.

Larry Freeman. *Grand Old American Bottles*. Century House, New York, n.d.

Julian H. Toulouse. *Bottle Makers and Their Marks*. Nelson, Nashville, 1971.

Stephen Van Rensselaer. *Early American Flasks*. Borden, Alhambra, n.d.

Richard Watson. *Bitters Bottles*. Nelson, Nashville, 1965.

Black and White Illustrations:
Christie, Manson & Wood, 36–37; The Coca-Cola Company, Atlanta, Georgia, USA, 72–73; Rex Elliott, Oregon, USA, 68 top; Mary Evans Picture Library, 30–31, 45, 58 right, 59 bottom, 67, 96, end papers; Charles Gardner, New London, Connecticut, USA, 39 bottom, 51 bottom; Glass Manufacturers' Federation, London, 6–7, 28–29, 43 bottom, 62–63 top, 87 top; Hamlyn Group Picture Library, 8–9, 9, 18, 22, 22–23, 26, 31, 34, 38 bottom, 39 top, 41, 44–45, 48, 49, 54–55, 56–57, 58 left, 60–61, 62–63 bottom, 64, 65 bottom, 68 bottom, 69, 76, 77, 80, 81, 83, 84–85 bottom, 85 bottom, 87 bottom, 88–89, 90, 91, 92; Hawthorn Books, New York, USA, 86 right; Mansell Collection, 59 top; Paul Popper Ltd., 8; Syndication International, 13, 93 left.

Colour Illustrations:
American Home, New York, USA, 14; Mary Evans Picture Library, 32, 71; Fratelli Fabbri Editori, Milan, Italy, 78, 79; Hamlyn Group Picture Library, 10–11, 15, 17, 20, 21, 24, 34, 42, 43, 46, 47, 66, 70, 74, 75; Seattle Art Museum, Washington, USA, 24–25.

Line Drawings: Peter Fitzjohn

Index

A LIVERPOOL surgeon, was asked some time ago, "How do you account for the great mortality amongst infants in this country." He replied, "One of the chief causes is the use of GIN, by *nursing mothers*." Not a few of our dissipated criminals may thank their mothers for *sowing the seeds* of their ruin in infancy."

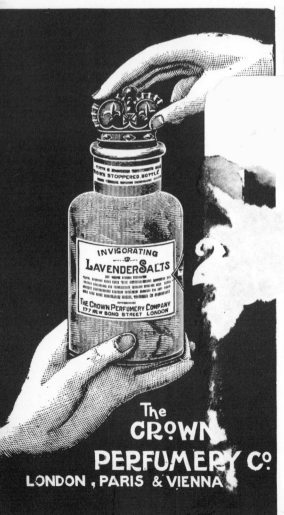
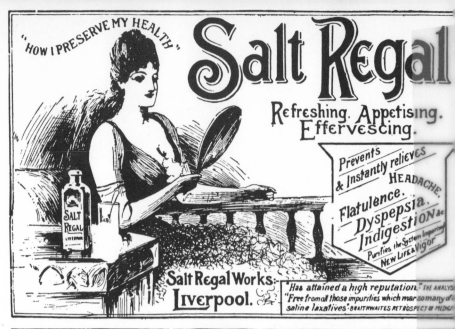